D0070201

EASY GUIDE TO
VOCABULARY

EASY GUIDE TO
VOCABULARY

FALL RIVER PRESS

New York

FALL RIVER PRESS

New York

An Imprint of Sterling Publishing
387 Park Avenue South
New York, NY 10016

FALL RIVER PRESS and the distinctive Fall River Press logo
are registered trademarks of Barnes & Noble, Inc.

© 2004, 2005 by Spark Publishing

All rights reserved. No part of this publication may be reproduced,
stored in a retrieval system, or transmitted in any form or by any means
(including electronic, mechanical, photocopying, recording, or otherwise)
without prior written permission from the publisher.

Text by Nina Rastogi

ISBN 978-1-4351-5426-1

For information about custom editions, special sales, and premium
and corporate purchases, please contact Sterling Special Sales at 800-805-5489
or specialsales@sterlingpublishing.com.

Manufactured in the United States of America

2 4 6 8 10 9 7 5 3 1

www.sterlingpublishing.com

CONTENTS

CONTENTS

CONTENTS

CONTENTS

I T ODUCTIO
SO YOU WANNA LEARN SOME VOCABULARY?

Makes sense. After all, having the proper vocabulary makes you sound smarter and feel more assured, and virtually guarantees you'll be a better writer and communicator. But who wants to slog through all those boring vocab lists? Or worse—use *flash cards*?! Please. I'd rather die. And anyhow, after you've gone through a thousand words in alphabetical order, how are you actually supposed to *remember* any of that stuff?

That's the point of this book—to fight the good fight against boring, yawn-worthy vocabulary training, and to do it in a way that helps you actually remember the words you *do* learn.

Ever go to a party where you were introduced to a ton of new people? Usually, the names you hear will go in one ear and right out the other—unless, of course, the person introducing you gives you a helpful little description of their friend. As in, "This is Sheila. She trains mountain goats and has a birthmark that bears a striking resemblance to the state of Kentucky." It's always easier to remember a person if you get to know a little bit about them, and the same thing goes for vocabulary words.

Easy Guide to Vocabulary introduces vocabulary words to you like a good party host. Each chapter starts with a story. The story is there to get you to picture certain characters, situations, or ideas. Then, once you've got that firmly implanted in your brain, the chapter goes on to introduce several words that follow those themes. That way, you'll attach words to concepts you've already learned, rather than being force-fed words in a random order. And because you're learning words that are grouped together thematically, you'll automatically be learning how those words are related to *one another*. Sneaky, huh? When you're done, you can take a test at the end of the chapter, and then congratulate yourself on how much you've picked up.

Oops! With all this talk about introducing, I forgot to introduce myself . . .

my name's Alex Lee, and I'll be your narrator today. I'm eighteen years old and in my senior year of high school. I write and perform poetry, and I have a dictator for a father and a pair of monkeys for brothers. I live in California, the state that has the most pop songs written about it (I'm not sure that's actually true, but I figure it has to be).

See? You'll never forget me. And now, on with the vocab!

EASY GUIDE TO
VOCABULARY

CHAPTER 1
HOW TO TALK ABOUT FAMILY MEMBERS

The alarm clock went off at 6:45, the same as it does every weekday. I rolled over and stared at the ceiling for a few moments as the clock kept blaring.

So this was what eighteen felt like.

I wiped the crud from my eyes and slammed the snooze button before flopping back into bed. In a few minutes I'd have to get up and get ready for school, but for right now I just wanted to lie in bed and wallow for a bit. Alex Lee, eighteen-year-old. It sounded strange, and I wasn't exactly sure how I felt about it.

The phone rang just then. Good old Janet, I thought. Wanted to be the first to wish me a happy birthday. I fumbled around for the handset, which had somehow gotten buried under a pile of laundry wadded up at the foot of my bed.

"Morning, darling," I mumbled, sleepily.

"Good morning, *Lee*," the voice crackled, underlining my last name gooily. "I hear it's your birthday."

"Ew, Walter? Walter Chen, is that you? Get off of my phone, you freak!" I clicked the phone off and tossed it back under the pile. Great, I thought. Now my big eighteenth was jinxed for sure. Walter Chen had been my nemesis since the eighth grade, when I beat him in the school spelling bee and he cried like a baby. Underneath all that slime is a great guy, I'm sure, but I for one have never had the benefit of witnessing it. With all the time he spends bothering me, I'm amazed he's able to keep up that 4.0 he's so proud of.

I stumbled down to the kitchen, briefly noting my appearance in the hall mirror. Fantastic. A wake-up call from Walter and a cowlick the size of the former Soviet Union. I tried to slick it down, but my hair was obviously having none of it. Ever since I shaved my head about a year ago, my hair had been growing back all weird and spiky (and no, not hot-supermodel spiky, more like eight-year-old-with-ADD spiky).

When I came down to the kitchen, my family was already there. Dad was standing, as always, at the kitchen counter, his daily cup of coffee (three sugars, splash of milk) halfway drunk, his English muffin crisped to perfection, the newspaper folded with razor precision to the business section. My twin brothers, Mike and Wayne, were sitting at the table, taking turns stuffing bananas up their noses.

"That's disgusting," I said, as I took out the orange juice.

"*You're* disgusting," said Mike. Wayne burst into laughter and high-fived him.

"Ew, are you *nine*?" I said as I rolled my eyes.

Mike and Wayne proceeded to pretend to sneeze out bananas in my direction. If only all those freshman girls could see them now, I thought.

"Morning, princess," my dad muttered distractedly.

I started to tell him that I was probably too old to be called "princess" anymore when he looked at his watch. "Shoot," he exclaimed. He gave me a quick kiss on the top of the head and ran out the door. "I'll be home late tonight, so you kids figure out dinner yourselves." Mike and Wayne high-fived each other again—dinner ourselves usually meant pizza from Papa John's™ and a liter of Coke each—and then ambled upstairs to get their stuff for class.

Oh, perfect. Just perfect. My eighteenth and no one remembered. Someone tell me, quick—when did my life become the plot of a bad Molly Ringwald movie? I sighed, polished off my orange juice, and headed upstairs to brush my teeth.

*   *   *   *   *

Now that you've read the story, take a look at the vocab words that relate to it. Pay attention to how the words are grouped. When you're done, try the exercises at the end of the chapter.

WORDS ABOUT ALEX

Like everyone else, I have a lot of **attributes** that make me who I am.

   attribute (*n*): a quality, property, or characteristic of somebody or something

RELATED WORDS

My brother's greatest **idiosyncrasy** is that he sometimes likes to bite his toenails.
    idiosyncrasy (*n*): an attribute that makes you different from other people

I have an **acerbic** wit: My grandmother used to say that if my tongue were any sharper, I'd cut myself on it.
    acerbic (*adj*): bitter or sharp in tone, taste, or manner

Some close synonyms for acerbic are **sardonic** (*adj*): disdainfully or ironically mocking, and **mordant** (*adj*): sharply sarcastic or bitingly critical.

I like to think of myself as an artist, with a keen sense of **aesthetics**.
    aesthetics (*n*): how something looks, especially when considered in terms of how pleasing it is

I've been a **prolific** writer ever since I was young—I've filled eight binders, three shoeboxes, and countless restaurant napkins with poetry.
    prolific (*adj*): highly productive

I'm **discerning** when it comes to literature, but apparently not when it comes to clothing. I like to put together crazy outfits, like ski parkas with tuxedo pants and pigtails. I told my friend Janet that that particular look was just **eclectic**, but she didn't buy it.
    discerning (*adj*): showing good taste and judgment
    eclectic (*adj*): made up of elements from various sources

I'm proud to dress the way I do! I'm not embarrassed to be an **iconoclast**!
    iconoclast (*n*): someone who challenges traditional beliefs, customs, and values

My fashion sense is definitely **heterodox**, but only boring people dress like they just stepped out of a J. Crew catalog.
    heterodox (*adj*): going against established or accepted beliefs or theories (traditionally used in terms of religion)

My room is usually completely **disheveled**—papers everywhere, laundry not folded. I'm amazed I can even find myself in all this mess.
    disheveled (*adj*): disordered and untidy

My father thinks my room is **deplorable**—he always says he's embarrassed to even look at it.
> **deplorable** (*adj*): worthy of severe condemnation

My dad thinks I'm too lazy for my own good. He sees me watching TV on the couch *once* and he assumes that I've sunk into a hopeless state of **lethargy**.
> **lethargy** (*n*): a state of physical slowness and mental dullness

My dad deplores my **lassitude** and my **torpor**, but I always tell him I'm simply in **repose**, storing up energy to go out and be productive.
> **lassitude** (*n*): a state of weariness accompanied by listlessness or apathy
> **torpor** (*n*): lack of mental or physical energy
> **repose** (*n*): state of rest or inactivity

My father thinks poetry is a waste of time; he thinks I'm **squandering** my talents.
> **squander** (*v*): to use something wastefully

He wants me to do something more **constructive** with my time—and by "constructive," he means "something that will get me into an Ivy League school."
> **constructive** (*adj*): involved in building, especially a foundation or base

WORDS ABOUT ALEX'S DAD

My dad once trained as an opera singer: When he turns on that big, deep voice, he seems totally **indomitable**.
> **indomitable** (*adj*): impossible to defeat or frighten

RELATED WORDS

My brothers think my father runs our house like a complete **autocrat**. I think he could be a lot more **imperious** than he actually is, but I have to agree that our house is a little too **authoritarian**.
> **autocrat** (*n*): a ruler who holds complete, unlimited power
> **imperious** (*adj*): haughty and domineering
> **authoritarian** (*adj*): favoring strict rules and established authority

My father's love for us is **indubitable**. His sanity, on the other hand—now that's another story.

> **indubitable** (*adj*): obviously true and not to be doubted

When my dad makes up his mind about something, he's totally **inexorable**. One time he decided we all had too much sugar in our diets, so he wouldn't let us eat anything but bran and spinach for a week.

> **inexorable** (*adj*): unstoppable

I was amazed at the way my father stuck **tenaciously** to the bran-and-spinach plan. Even when my brothers threatened to stop eating entirely, he remained **imperturbable**.

> **tenaciously** (*adv*): sticking firmly to a decision or plan
> **imperturbable** (*adj*): not easily worried or distressed

My father is always complaining about my messy room, but honestly! He's so **meticulous** that he color-codes his sock drawer. And his shoes. And his closet. And his bookshelves. . . .

> **meticulous** (*adj*): extremely careful and precise

Some synonyms for **meticulous** are:

> **conscientious** (*adj*): thorough and careful in one's work
> **punctilious** (*adj*): being careful about small details
> **immaculate** (*adj*): completely clean
> **scrupulous** (*adj*): very precise and exact

I know I should show my father more **deference**, but, after all, it's *my* life!

> **deference** (*n*): submission to another's judgment, opinions, or wishes

My dad is a total **zealot** about getting me to go to college.

> **zealot** (*n*): somebody who shows excessive enthusiasm for a cause (usually in a religious sense)

One of the major **tenets** of my father's belief system is that a good education will get you anywhere you want in the world.

> **tenet** (*n*): one of a set of fundamental beliefs

Because my father is such a zealot—and since he pays for everything in the house—my brothers and I have to accept his ideas as **dogma**.

> **dogma** (*n*): an authoritative stand that all believers must accept as correct

All my dad's scary qualities **belie** a very loving, supportive nature.
  belie (*v*): to disguise the true nature of something

WORDS ABOUT ALEX'S BROTHERS

My brothers are typical fifteen-year-old boys: they have the most **asinine** senses of humor.
  asinine (*adj*): totally stupid or ridiculous (Literally, it means "like an ass!" How's that for a memory device?)

My brothers are totally **apathetic** about my interests. But then again, I've never gone to see them play football, so I guess I can't complain.
  apathetic (*adj*): not taking any interest in anything

I think it's really true what they say about twins: Mike and Wayne both get really **petulant** when the other is gone for too long.
  petulant (*adj*): bad-tempered and sulky, like a child

My brothers like to rip on substitute teachers who are too **credulous**. They love that old switching-seats-and-pretending-to-be-each-other routine.
  credulous (*adj*): gullible; believing something too easily

When my brothers were just **neophytes** in high school, they used to ask me lots of questions about how it all worked. Now that they're Misters Big and Popular, they barely acknowledge my presence.
  neophyte (*n*): beginner (This word was traditionally used in a religious sense; a *neophyte* was someone who had just joined a religious community— say, a monastery—but hadn't taken vows yet.)

No matter how much I complain about them, though, my brothers are pretty **benign**; they've never teamed up on me too badly.
  benign (*adj*): gentle, nonthreatening, mild

RELATED WORDS

innocuous (*adj*): harmless

My brothers aren't just popular because they like to make asses of themselves. They're also really friendly and **convivial** (just not to their older sister).

convivial (*adj*): enjoying the company of others
genial (*adj*): having a kind, good-natured manner
jovial (*adj*): cheerful
blithe (*adj*): happy and carefree
risible (*adj*): capable of causing laughter

There's no real **animosity** between us. In general, we get along pretty well.

animosity (*n*): feeling of hostility

YOUR TURN

Match the vocab words on the left with their definitions on the right.

1.	eclectic	a.	sharp
2.	acerbic	b.	innocent
3.	authoritarian	c.	messy
4.	immaculate	d.	able to make people laugh
5.	punctilious	e.	very clean
6.	neophyte	f.	hard-core believer
7.	risible	g.	beginner
8.	innocuous	h.	strict
9.	disheveled	i.	taken from many different sources
10.	zealot	j.	concerned about small details

In each of the groups below, choose the word that does not belong.

11. genial   mordant   jovial   blithe
12. meticulous   scrupulous   disheveled   punctilious
13. obedience   deference   defiance   submission
14. benign   harmless   innocuous   threatening
15. imperturbable   petulant   cranky   irritable

Choose the word that best completes the sentence.

16. Big sisters are often very _____ toward their younger siblings
    (A) mordant (B) petulant (C) imperious (D) asinine

17. On Monday mornings, I'm usually overcome by _____; I can
    hardly get out of bed.
    (A) dogma (B) lethargy (C) anathema (D) attribute

18. Britney Spears is a(n) _____ artist—she always seems to be
    coming out with new albums.
    (A) heterodox (B) aesthetic (C) indomitable (D) prolific

19. It is a(n) _____ fact that January always follows December.
    (A) indubitable (B) deplorable (C) genial (D) discerning

20. Whatever you think about him, you have to admit that Michael Jackson is a complete _____. He's like no one else on Earth!
    (A) zealot (B) iconoclast (C) tenet (D) neophyte

21. The selection on TV tonight is utterly _____. I guess I'll have to go out to see a movie instead.
    (A) parochial (B) deplorable (C) discerning (D) immaculate

22. The atmosphere at the party was _____; no one could resist having a good time.
    (A) asinine (B) conscientious (C) meticulous (D) convivial

23. My strangest _____ is that I sometimes like to put garlic powder on my vanilla ice cream.
    (A) torpor (B) aesthetic (C) idiosyncrasy (D) tenet

24. Sometimes people mistake my _____ wit for mean-spiritedness.
    (A) sardonic (B) heterodox (C) imperturbable (D) blithe

25. I'm not very _____ about my room: I just sort of throw things wherever.
    (A) jovial (B) eclectic (C) constructive (D) meticulous

CHAPTER 2
HOW TO TALK ABOUT SCHOOL

"*No* one remembered? Not even your dad?"

"Nope, not even my dad," I said, as I unwrapped my cafeteria burrito. I poked around in it with my finger. "What the hell is this, anyway?"

"Ew, don't touch it, just eat it," said Janet.

"Seriously, is this even legal?" I asked, as I flung what I assumed was a bean at her face.

She giggled and picked the mystery food piece out of her hair before tossing it back at me. "Hey, you be nice to that burrito. You know, there are starving children in Africa who would kill for a prime Westerburg High burrito like the one you have there."

"Then they're welcome to it." She giggled again and closed up her calculus textbook. Janet was taking AP Calc, AP Bio, and fifth-year Spanish, and could usually be found studying over lunch. She was also the editor-in-chief of the newspaper and captain of the girls' field hockey team, and had never worn braces in her life. She was, in my father's words, "a good influence." Lucky for her I never held that against her. I decided to forego the rest of the burrito and balled up the wrapper.

"You wouldn't be thinking of leaving that on the table now, would you, Lee?" That oily, irritating voice could only mean one thing.

"Not a chance, Mr. Limbergh. I was just making my way over to the trash can."

A small, rodentlike face popped out from behind our principal's considerable stomach. "None of your lip, Lee!" it screeched.

"Sure thing, Mr. Quimby, sir."

The vice-principal narrowed his beady little eyes at me, and both he and Mr. Limbergh kept their eyes firmly locked on me as I slowly walked to the row of garbage cans.

Limbergh and Quimby don't like me, and that's an understatement. They like to think they run this school like their own private military compound, and they hate—*hate*—people who talk back. Last year they'd caved to parent pressure to ban *Catcher in the Rye* from the English curriculum, and I raised a stink about it in an editorial for the *Tatler*. I mean, I find Holden Caulfield as annoying as the next guy, but that doesn't mean the book should be *banned*. Man, I can't *wait* to leave all this high school crap behind, I thought as I walked back to the picnic table. I don't hate the *idea* of school. Just the reality of high school.

Limbergh and Quimby gave a nod to Janet—honestly, I think she's the only reason they haven't managed to suspend me yet—and went to go rout out the potheads smoking in the girls' room.

"Well, that was exciting." She finished off her pudding cup and threw it in her lunch bag. "Hey, I know what we could do for your birthday."

"What? Something glamorous, I hope."

"Sure. There's a pep rally tonight."

"Ew!" I screeched. "Not a chance in hell."

"Come *on*, Alex. If we get to June and you've never gone to a pep rally, I don't think they can give you your diploma."

I rolled my eyes. "Fine. But only because *Buffy* is a rerun."

"Great. I'll pick you up at six."

Fantastic. Best birthday ever.

*   *   *   *   *

WORDS ABOUT HIGH SCHOOL

High school fashion is really **capricious**: one week it's all wallet chains, dog collars, and low riders, and then the next it's Gap khakis and polo shirts.

    capricious (*adj*): tending to make sudden, unpredictable changes

The popular crowd has an amazing power to **assimilate** other people: If you start hanging out with them, pretty soon you're dressing, walking, and talking like them.

    assimilate (*v*): to integrate into a group so that differences are erased

My journalistic right to free speech was really **constrained** by the principal, who didn't think my editorial was appropriate for a school paper.

constrain (*v*): to limit or restrict something

RELATED WORDS

A close synonym is **circumscribe** (*v*): to limit the power of something or somebody. In math terms, to *circumscribe* a geometric shape means drawing another shape around it so they touch at every corner—think of a circle ("circum-") being drawn (or "scribed") around a square.

In your senior year, English, math, and a foreign language are **compulsory** subjects.

compulsory (*adj*): required by law or authority

State law **compels** me to stay in high school till I turn eighteen, and there's no way I can **coerce** my father into letting me homeschool myself.

compel (*v*): to make something happen by force

coerce (*v*): to force someone to do something (usually implies persuasion)

Most students at my high school only do a **cursory** job on their homework; they don't bother really learning anything.

cursory (*adj*): done quickly or superficially

I'm so bored by the **quotidian** nature of high school! Why does nothing exciting ever happen?

quotidian (*adj*): ordinary, everyday

Someday, I will look back on high school and think fondly of these **halcyon** days. Unfortunately, that day is not today.

halcyon (*adj*): peaceful, free from disturbance

High school girls can be really **disingenuous**: They'll fawn over you to your face, and then, as soon as your back is turned, they'll dis you.

disingenuous (*adj*): giving a false impression of sincerity

WORDS ABOUT JANET

SCHOOL

Janet is completely **indefatigable**; she's president of four clubs, captain of the field hockey team, and manages to pull straight A's—and she never takes naps!
> **indefatigable** (*adj*): never showing signs of tiredness

My father admires Janet's **intrepid** struggle to get into the best college she can.
> **intrepid** (*adj*): brave; persistent in the pursuit of something

Teachers love Janet's **assiduousness** when it comes to her homework.
> **assiduousness** (*n*): care, effort

I've never seen Janet get in trouble for anything—she's completely **irreproachable**.
> **irreproachable** (*adj*): unable to be criticized

Janet is really **judicious** with her compliments, so you know you can always take what she says at face value.
> **judicious** (*adj*): showing wisdom and good sense, especially in the sense of avoiding unnecessary trouble or waste

RELATED WORDS

Here are some synonyms for **judicious**:
> **sagacious** (*adj*): very knowledgeable and intelligent, showing good judgment
> **astute** (*adj*): shrewd, discerning
> **discriminating** (*adj*): able to judge very subtle differences

Janet is positively **munificent** with her time, energy, and support.
> **munificent** (*adj*): very generous

Janet's **magnanimity** knows no bounds: She devotes a lot of her spare time to **altruistic** causes like volunteering and tutoring.
> **magnanimity** (*n*): generosity
> **altruistic** (*adj*): showing concern for others

Janet will someday grow up to be a great president or a major business **magnate**.
> **magnate** (*n*): somebody with a lot of wealth and power

Most teachers hold Janet up as a **paragon** of excellence in the classroom.
paragon (*n*): somebody or something who is the best example of something

Some kids at school like to imply that Janet is an **opportunist**—they just can't understand that she does all this stuff because she genuinely cares, not because she's trying to get something out of it.
opportunist (*n*): somebody who takes advantage of something—particularly someone who does so in a dishonest or unethical way

WORDS ABOUT THE ADMINISTRATORS

SCHOOL

Mr. Quimby is such a **martinet**, I bet he'd make a great drill sergeant.
martinet (*n*): someone who imposes strict discipline on others

RELATED WORDS

Sometimes Mr. Quimby goes on these **despotic** rampages and does random things like canceling off-campus lunch privileges for no reason.
despotic (*adj*): behaving like a tyrant

Mr. Limbergh is so **pedantic**; he gets really irritated if the morning announcements start at 8:07 instead of 8:05.
pedantic (*adj*): too concerned with the correct rules and details

Mr. Quimby is so **irascible** around teenagers; it makes me wonder why he got into education in the first place.
irascible (*adj*): easily moved to anger

Mr. Quimby likes to use **insipid** sayings, such as "The early bird gets the worm." But really, who wants a worm in the first place?
insipid (*adj*): dull, unoriginal

Sometimes I think Mr. Quimby's only job on campus is to **mollify** Mr. Limbergh when he gets all ticked off.
mollify (*v*): to soothe

Mr. Quimby speaks in this really annoying, **querulous** voice that only a Chihuahua could love.
querulous (*adj*): whiny or complaining

Mr. Limbergh likes to **relegate** less savory duties—like bathroom patrol—to Mr. Quimby.
relegate (*v*): to pass responsibility for something onto someone else

Mr. Quimby is such a **sycophant**—think Burns and Mr. Smithers from *The Simpsons* and you'll get a pretty good picture.
sycophant (*n*): someone who sickeningly flatters a superior

Mr. Quimby is so **compliant** to everything Mr. Limbergh says. I wish he'd have an original opinion, just once!
compliant (*adj*): easily agreeing or conforming

A synonym for *compliant* is **tractable** (*adj*): very easy to control.

Mr. Limbergh is really **supercilious** around the students—but I think it probably comes from the fear of being exposed as a huge moron.
supercilious (*adj*): contemptuous and arrogant

Mr. Quimby would like to see himself as a cool, **stolid** guy, but he gets so flustered at the tiniest problems.
stolid (*adj*): solemn, emotionless

If it hadn't been for Janet coming in at exactly the right time, Mr. Limbergh would have never granted me any **clemency**.
clemency (*n*): an act of mercy or leniency

Eventually I was **exonerated** of my supposed **infraction**, but not until Janet could **corroborate** my story that I had, in fact, passed the editorial by our faculty advisor. Honestly—this administration treats a little freethinking as if it were an act of supreme **heresy**!

exonerate (*v*): to officially declare someone not guilty

infraction (*n*): an instance of breaking the law

corroborate (*v*): to back up someone's story, to show that something is true

heresy (*n*): an opinion that contradicts established theory (originally used in a religious sense to mean an act or statement that went against the established religious beliefs)

Mr. Quimby is such a **misanthrope**, it's no wonder he's still single.

misanthrope (*n*): someone who hates people

Mr. Quimby likes to clear his throat before he launches into his **bombastic**, moralizing speeches.

bombastic (*adj*): long-winded and pretentious, with the intent of impressing people

Mr. Quimby once issued an **injunction** that all students had to start addressing him as Your Grand Excellence.

injunction (*n*): a command from someone in a position of authority

Mr. Limbergh **patronizes** us like we're a bunch of eight-year-olds.

patronize (*v*): to talk down to someone

Our administration is so **parochial**. It couldn't care less what is happening in the Middle East, as long as the campus is clean and we send a bunch of kids off to the Ivy League again.

parochial (*adj*): concerned only with local issues, without regard to the wider world

I probably shouldn't be so **contemptuous** of our administrators—it's not their fault they're morons.

contemptuous (*adj*): feeling or expressing a strong dislike or disrespect

Quimby hates nothing in the world as much as he hates **insolent** students.

insolent (*adj*): showing a lack of respect

SCHOOL

YOUR TURN

Match the vocab words on the left with the word or phrase that means the opposite on the right.

1.	magnanimous	a.	stingy
2.	cursory	b.	honest
3.	contemptuous	c.	even-tempered
4.	judicious	d.	admiring
5.	compulsory	e.	wasteful
6.	mollify	f.	not required
7.	astute	g.	to make someone angry
8.	exonerate	h.	to condemn
9.	irascible	i.	in-depth
10.	disingenuous	j.	dull

In each of the groups below, choose the word that does not belong.

11. judicious   unintelligent   astute   sagacious
12. greedy   altruistic   munificent   generous
13. tractable   compliant   stubborn   obedient
14. indefatigable   tireless   intrepid   lazy
15. quotidian   inspired   boring   insipid

Choose the word that best completes the sentence.

16. Whenever I don't want to do a particular thing, I try to _____ the job to one of my younger brothers.

    (A) constrain (B) corroborate (C) relegate (D) circumscribe

17. I've always found Chris Rock to be a(n) _____ of humor. He cracks me up!

    (A) paragon (B) misanthrope (C) martinet (D) opportunist

18. Last summer I spent ten _____ days in Hawaii—no phones, no email, and no television.
(A) pedantic (B) quotidian (C) altruistic (D) halcyon

19. When I wanted to go see the Strokes concert last month, I told my dad I was studying at Janet's house. Luckily, when my dad called over there, Janet's mom _____ our story and he never found out.
(A) corroborated (B) patronized (C) mollified (D) exonerated

20. If my dad ever found out, though, there's no way I'd be granted any _____. I'd be grounded for life for sure.
(A) clemency (B) paragon (C) heresy (D) bombast

21. My cousin's latest short story is totally _____, but I suppose you can't blame her; she is eight, after all.
(A) tractable (B) insipid (C) assiduous (D) sagacious

22. Watch out—Mr. Quimby will give you detention for even the tiniest _____.
(A) heresy (B) coercion (C) exoneration (D) infraction

23. If you want to play a sport at my school, it is _____ that you maintain a 2.75 GPA.
(A) pedantic (B) stolid (C) compulsory (D) insolent

24. When presidential candidates speak on TV, they're often loud and _____.
(A) cursory (B) bombastic (C) halcyon (D) munificent

25. I was a pretty careful, cautious kid when I was little; my brothers, on the other hand, have always been silly and _____.
(A) capricious (B) parochial (C) compulsory (D) disingenuous

SCHOOL

CHAPTER 3
HOW TO TALK ABOUT SPORTS AND ATHLETES

"Okay, I'm here, but I refuse to do the wave. First sign of the wave and I bolt."

"Fine, Alex. I don't think anyone even *does* the wave anymore."

We were sitting under a large banner that read "Westerburg Wildcats." Janet was dressed in the Westerburg colors—mustard and violet, a combination even she didn't pull off very well—and was shaking a big foam finger. I was bundled up in an old Boredoms hoodie and trying to sink lower into the bleacher. "It's freezing," I mumbled. "No, it's not, Alex. It's California," she said.

I peered down over the railing into a sea of mustard-and-violet-clad cheerleaders. Tara Mickleson, the head cheerleader, was pulling off a rather remarkable set of cartwheels. When she righted herself, I thought I saw a cloud of hair spray rise off her head. "Amazing! Did you see that? Her ponytail didn't even *budge*."

Janet started to laugh and then socked me on the shoulder. "Be nice! She's really sweet. We're on Winter Ball committee together." Funny, Tara and I were lab partners in the eighth grade. I remember she really had a thing for unicorns back then—every inch of her Trapper Keeper was covered with stickers of them. Sometimes I'm really tempted to ask her what happened to that thing.

"Look, there are your brothers." I followed Janet's hand and saw them standing near the snack shack, surrounded by their usual freshman posse. Janet put two fingers in her mouth and whistled at them. Mike pretended to faint when he saw me in the stands, so I flipped him off and stuck my tongue out. Wayne caught my imaginary finger and stuck it in his back pocket, which made all the girls laugh like they'd never, ever seen anyone do that before.

The game started and Janet got really caught up in it—but not *so* caught up that she didn't notice when I pulled out my Discman, unfortunately, so I sheepishly stuck it back in my coat. I watched for a while, then got bored and allowed my eyes to wander over the crowd. All the faces in the stands were glowing from

23

the stadium lights. If I tuned out all the noise, it was a really beautiful picture. I was trying to work at the image—maybe it would turn up in my next poem—when all of a sudden my eyes landed on something worth looking at.

"Oh ho," I muttered under my breath. "*Hell*--o."

He was sitting alone in the top row, hands jammed in the pockets of his beat-up leather coat. His hair was falling in that perfect, I-didn't-mean-to-do-this, indie-rocker flop around his eyes. I looked down and—be still my beating heart—he was wearing old-school black Converse sneakers.

Janet noticed that my attention had wandered. She raised an eyebrow.

"Who is that total *fox* over there?" I whispered breathlessly.

"Tell me you didn't just seriously use the word *fox*."

"Shut up, Gonzales. Who is he? Do you know?"

She looked at him again. "New guy, I guess."

He must have noticed the two of us staring like idiots, because at that moment he looked over and smiled—at least, I think it was a smile.

Well . . . maybe year eighteen was going to be exciting after all.

* * * * *

WORDS ABOUT SCHOOL SPIRIT

Janet told me we had to go to the pep rally to **bolster** the football team.

bolster (*v*): to strengthen or support something

RELATED WORDS

A very close synonym for bolster is *buttress*. *Buttress* can also be used as a noun: something that supports a larger structure.

Sometimes the **ardor** of football fans scares me.

ardor (*n*): intense feeling

Here are some synonyms for **ardor**:

> **fervor** (*n*): extreme emotion or belief (sometimes you'll see this word as
> > **fervency**)
>
> **fanaticism** (*n*): extreme enthusiasm or belief

The difference between the two is that a **fanatic** takes his or her **fervor** too far—**fanaticism** usually implies irrationality and a lack of clear thinking.

The stadium was filled with **ebullient** people, screaming and clapping for their team.

> **ebullient** (*adj*): full of cheerful enthusiasm

My brothers were in a state of **euphoria** at the pep rally; they were so filled with **exuberance** that they gave shouts of **exultation**.

> **euphoria** (*n*): a feeling of great joy
>
> **exuberance** (*n*): cheerful enthusiasm
>
> **exultation** (*n*): a feeling of great joy or triumph, or the expression of that
> > feeling

I, however, remained **aloof** during the whole thing. I'm far too dignified to do the wave.

> **aloof** (*adj*): unwilling to get involved, usually out of a sense of superiority

Janet, however, felt the **compulsion** to whoop it up with the rest of the crowd.

> **compulsion** (*n*): a force that makes someone do something

I don't see how Janet and I can be such good friends, given my **aversion** to school spirit events.

> **aversion** (*n*): strong feeling of dislike

I can't get into all this **frivolity**—really, I have better things to do than yell for a dumb football game.

> **frivolity** (*n*): silly or trivial behavior

I will admit, though—I do like the feeling of **camaraderie** at these things.

> **camaraderie** (*n*): a feeling of closeness among a particular group of people

I like the way it makes our school feel **cohesive**.

> **cohesive** (*adj*): sticking together

My brothers got mad at me for **fraternizing** with someone from the other team—even though I've known him forever from band camp.

> **fraternize** (*v*): to socialize with other people—especially people with whom you shouldn't be friendly

I'm not sure what these pep rallies are supposed to **nurture**—camaraderie among your classmates, or fanatic hatred for the opposing team.

> **nurture** (*v*): to encourage something to grow

WORDS ABOUT CHEERLEADERS

One of cheerleaders wears this little Hello Kitty headband that I find really **cloying**.

> **cloying** (*adj*): sickeningly sweet

Cheerleaders have to be incredibly friendly and **effervescent**—it all seems awfully tiring.

> **effervescent** (*adj*): lively, bubbly

RELATED WORDS

A synonym for *effervescent* is **vivacious** (*adj*): lively, high-spirited.

Most cheerleaders are really **gregarious**; it's rare to meet a shy cheerleader.

> **gregarious** (*adj*): friendly, sociable, talkative

If you are too **loquacious**, you might be **garrulous**.

> **loquacious** (*adj*): friendly, sociable, talkative (a synonym for *gregarious*)
> **garrulous** (*adj*): excessively talkative

Listening to cheerleaders **prattle** on about the game was giving me a headache.

> **prattle** (*v*): to talk in a silly, childish way

Prattle can also be used as a noun: The cheerleaders' constant **prattle** drove me bonkers.

SPORTS AND ATHLETES

From way up in the bleachers, the cheerleading squad looked quite **homogenous**: They all had on matching uniforms, and they even had matching hairdos and sneakers.

> **homogenous** (*adj*): being similar in nature (the prefix *homo* means "alike" or "the same")

The cheerleaders' **conformity** scared me a little. I wonder if they move, talk, and dress the same way off the field too. . . .

> **conformity** (*n*): behavior that completely complies with accepted standards. The word has a definite negative connotation—it implies dullness and unthinking behavior.

The **incessant**, repetitive cheers were beginning to grind on my nerves.

> **incessant** (*adj*): nonstop

The loudspeaker was **stridently** broadcasting the cheers across the whole neighborhood.

> **strident** (*adj*): loud, harsh in tone

The head cheerleader is in math with me. It's amazing that a girl who's so vivacious on the field can be so **vapid** in class.

> **vapid** (*adj*): dull, lacking interest

I think all that jumping and squealing is really pretty **inane**.

> **inane** (*adj*): senseless, unimportant

Some synonyms for *inane* are **vacuous** (*adj*): lacking intelligence or content and **fatuous** (*adj*): unintelligent and unaware.

I should probably stop **vilifying** cheerleaders. After all, they're actually *doing* something with their time, right?

> **vilify** (*v*): to say abusive things about someone else

I should just keep all these nasty, **derisive** comments to myself.

> **derisive** (*adj*): showing contempt

SPORTS AND ATHLETES

WORDS ABOUT ATHLETES AND COMPETITION

The football players were quick and **adroit**. There's no way I could ever handle a ball like that.

> **adroit** (*adj*): quick and skillful, either physically or mentally

RELATED WORDS

Two synonyms for *adroit* are **dexterous** (*adj*) and **agile** (*adj*).

Some of the bigger athletes moved **ponderously** across the field, weighed down by all their padding.

> **ponderously** (*adv*): in a lumbering, slow, and heavy manner

Despite his **prodigious** bulk, however, the biggest guy on the field was quite agile.

> **prodigious** (*adj*): great in amount or size

Personally, I prefer brains over **brawn** in a guy.

> **brawn** (*n*): physical strength

Each of the athletes has such a great **physique**. Hmm, maybe I should start jogging again.

> **physique** (*n*): the shape and size of someone's body

One of the quarterbacks was a total **novice**: He was so nervous, I was afraid he was going to throw up in his helmet.

> **novice** (*n*): someone who is new at something

Tonight we were playing our greatest **adversary**, Monte Vista High School.

> **adversary** (*n*): opponent

A synonym for *adversary* is **antagonist** (*n*)). The term comes from literature, where an *antagonist* is a character whose goals, values, or behavior conflict with the **protagonist** (*n*): the main character in a work of literature.

There's a lot of **enmity** between Westerburg and Monte Vista.

    enmity (*n*): hatred

I was afraid an **altercation** was going to break out when the referee gave the point to the other team.

    altercation (*n*): heated argument

The intense game really **polarized** the two halves of the audience.

    polarize (*v*): to make the differences between groups clearer and more extreme

My brothers' admiration for the star quarterback borders on **idolatry**.

    idolatry (*n*): fanatical worship of something or somebody

I think he's a **narcissistic** pig: he always acts like he won the game single-handedly and never bothers to give his teammates any credit.

    narcissistic (*adj*): excessively self-admiring or self-centered. The term comes from the Greek myth of Narcissus, a beautiful young man who fell in love with his own reflection.

YOUR TURN

Match the vocab words on the left with their definitions on the right.

1.	compulsion	a.	fight
2.	adroit	b.	talkative
3.	prodigious	c.	skillful
4.	homogenous	d.	sticking together as a group
5.	cohesive	e.	separated
6.	polarize	f.	large; numerous
7.	nurture	g.	strong dislike
8.	loquacious	h.	force
9.	altercation	i.	all sharing the same characteristics
10.	aversion	j.	to encourage

In each of the groups below, choose the word that does not belong.

11. bolster   support   weaken   buttress
12. ardor   aloofness   ebullience   fervor
13. boredom   euphoria   exultation   joy
14. vilify   deride   praise   mock
15. garrulous   gregarious   talkative   silent

Choose the word that best completes the sentence.

16. In order to be an MTV VJ, you need to have a lively, _____ personality.
    (A) cohesive (B) incessant (C) effervescent (D) inane

17. My skinny little brothers could never be considered _____, although they've been spending lots of time at the gym lately.
    (A) strident (B) brawny (C) aloof (D) derisive

18. I hate those _____ guys who are always checking themselves out in every reflective surface they pass.
    (A) dexterous (B) euphoric (C) vivacious (D) narcissistic

SPORTS AND ATHLETES

19. I'm a terrible babysitter, because I have no patience for the silly
    _____ of children.

    (A) prattle (B) ardor (C) antagonist (D) idolatry

20. Janet and I went to a beginners' pottery class, which was designed for total

    _____.

    (A) adversaries (B) novices (C) antagonists (D) exuberance

21. I don't like the way campaign advertisements always go out of their way to
    _____ the opponent.

    (A) vilify (B) polarize (C) prattle (D) bolster

22. In an effort to resist _____, I've taken to wearing two different-
    colored socks wherever I go.

    (A) euphoria (B) idolatry (C) brawn (D) conformity

23. My stupid brothers like to watch really _____ television shows like
    Punk'd.

    (A) garrulous (B) incessant (C) inane (D) ponderous

24. When I was thirteen, I exhibited a(n) _____ for the Backstreet
    Boys that highly embarrasses me now.

    (A) fanaticism (B) frivolity (C) camaraderie (D) dexterity

25. If you play basketball, chances are you're quite _____.

    (A) cloying (B) vivacious (C) agile (D) exuberant

SPORTS AND ATHLETES

CHAPTER 4
HOW TO TALK ABOUT THE BARE NECESSITIES

"Okay, spill it, Gonzales. What have you learned?"

It was Thursday night, which meant I was on duty at MFC, Mississippi Fried Chicken—"Home of the Big Wing." This was not exactly my first choice for an after-school job. I don't know about you, but I'm not crazy about fluorescent lighting and deep fryers. Still, there's not much out there for an eighteen-year-old who hates children (which rules out babysitting). I'm hoping it'll be character building—you know, give me real-world experience to put in my first novel.

Janet was sitting under the big cardboard "If It's Chicken, You're Lickin'" sign that was twisting aimlessly in the air-conditioning. She had her Stanford application material spread out in front of her, and she was desperately scribbling on a legal pad.

"I told you, Alex, I haven't heard anything yet. All I know is he's new, his name is Rex, and he's the year below us. I think he plays in a band."

"You're kidding me!" I shrieked. "A *band*? What kind of band? A good band? I *love* guys in bands!"

Janet giggled. "Yes, I know. And no, I don't know what kind of band it is."

I adjusted my hairnet. "I can't believe you didn't hear anything else."

"You know, Alex," Janet sighed, "I *do* have a life outside being your personal private investigator. I have all these to do." She gestured at the papers in front of her.

"Oh my God, Janet. I mean, aren't you done yet? Haven't you filled out, like, fourteen of those already? Can't you stop yet?"

She frowned. "Alex, this is my future we're talking about, you know? I want to make absolutely sure."

I pulled a bag of chicken nuggets out of the freezer. "God, you sound like my dad."

"Well, your dad is a smart guy, Alex. I mean, have you even *started* your

33

apps?" I mumbled something as I dumped the nuggets into the fryer. "Promise me you'll at least start on your essays, Alex."

"Fine, fine! I'll start them tonight."

"Behind on apps, Lee?" rang out an oozing voice, as the door banged open. Walter walked up to the counter and whipped a coupon out from his jacket pocket. "Says here I get a free Jumbotron drink with my order." I took the coupon grudgingly and got him his food as quickly as possible.

"Thanks and have a good night," I mumbled—but only because they make us say that.

"Thanks, Lee." He fished around in his pocket again. "By the way, you guys should stop by." He pushed a postcard across the counter at me.

"What is this, like, a math team party?" I scowled.

He rolled his eyes. "No, it's a concert. My cousin Rex is new in town, and his band is playing at the Tin Cup this weekend." He took his food, tipped his baseball cap to Janet, and headed out the door.

Uh-oh. Did this mean I was going to have to start being nice to *Walter*?

* * * * *

WORDS ABOUT FOOD

THE BARE NECESSITIES

Every evening after work, I come home with the **pungent** smell of fried chicken in my hair and clothing.

pungent (*adj*): strong smelling

RELATED WORDS

The following words can be used to describe the way something smells.

The **piquant** smells of the pumpkin pie left the whole kitchen **redolent** of Thanksgiving—that is, until my **malodorous** brother walked in and ruined everything with the **fetid** smell of his **rancid** old gym socks.

> **piquant** (*adj*): tasting or smelling savory or spicy
>
> **redolent** (*adj*): having a strong, pleasing smell. It can also mean suggestive or reminiscent of something.
>
> **malodorous** (*adj*): bad smelling. You can guess the meaning of this word by breaking it apart—*mal* means "bad" in Latin, and *odorous* means "smelling."
>
> **fetid** (*adj*): smelling rotten
>
> **rancid** (*adj*): tasting or smelling rotten

When my dad goes out of town, my brothers and I eat nothing but ramen noodles. It's our only **sustenance**.

> **sustenance** (*n*): something—especially food—that sustains life

My father is a real **epicurean**—he's ashamed to have a daughter who works at such an awful restaurant.

> **epicurean** (*n*): someone who takes pleasure in luxurious things, especially good food

The following two words also describe particular kinds of eaters.

If you're not careful, my brothers will eat anything in sight. They say they're **gourmands**, but I think they're just a couple of **gluttons**.

> **gourmand** (*n*): someone who loves food, and often eats too much
>
> **glutton** (*n*): someone who eats and drinks to excess

Glutton has a much more negative meaning than *gourmand*.

Mississippi Fried Chicken's corn on the cob is merely **palatable**, but the mashed potatoes are truly **delectable.** Don't believe the **succulent** pictures of chicken in our ads though. Our chicken is really as dry as bone.

> **palatable** (*adj*): acceptable tasting
>
> **delectable** (*adj*): delicious
>
> **succulent** (*adj*): juicy and delicious

All that fried food left **oleaginous** spots on my clean, new apron.

> **oleaginous** (*adj*): oily

The food at our restaurant is truly **abysmal**—even my brothers avoid it.

> **abysmal** (*adj*): completely awful

THE BARE NECESSITIES

Our favorite game at work is watching the fat at the bottom of the fryer **coagulate** into interesting shapes.

    coagulate (*v*): to thicken into a semisolid mass

In the United States, the **consumption** of alcohol is forbidden for people under the age of twenty-one.

    consumption (*n*): eating or drinking

If I ate all my meals at MFC, I would grow truly **corpulent**.

    corpulent (*adj*): fat

Sometimes I like to dare my coworkers to eat the **dregs** of chicken left at the bottom of the fryer.

    dreg (*n*): a small remainder of something

WORDS ABOUT WORK

Dumping big bags of chicken into the deep fryer all day is **arduous** work—but at least I'm developing nice, big arm muscles.

    arduous (*adj*): requiring hard work

RELATED WORDS

THE BARE NECESSITIES

Moving boxes up and down the stairs is also **strenuous** and **laborious** work, but it's not an overly **onerous** task. I kind of like it actually.

strenuous (*adj*) and **laborious** (*adj*) are synonyms for *arduous*.

    onerous (*adj*): also means "requiring great effort," but it has the added negative meaning of being a burden or a lot of trouble.

Refilling the ketchup bottles is the most **stultifying** task—there are so many of them!

    stultifying (*adj*): boring, tedious

I can't think of a more **mundane** job than the one I have.

    mundane (*adj*): boring and everyday

My father thinks that having an after-school job is an **unparalleled** learning experience.

    unparalleled (*adj*): unable to be matched

Every evening I **diligently** wipe down the countertops. My manager freaks out if I miss any little spot of chicken grease.

    diligently (*adv*): carefully, with a lot of effort

Just because she doesn't have to wear this stupid chicken hat, my manager feels justified in acting really **haughty** to all of us.

    haughty (*adj*): cocky, arrogant

Even though I only work four-hour shifts, an evening at MFC always seems **interminable**.

    interminable (*adj*): unending

As much as I complain about it, there is something really **gratifying** about making your own money.

    gratifying (*adj*): pleasing, satisfying

They other day, though, I **malingered** in order to stay home and watch the MTV Video Music Awards.

    malinger (*v*): to pretend to be sick, especially to avoid work

I thought my coworker was going to spill the beans about my **truancy**, but luckily I was able to bribe him by taking over bathroom duty the next night.

    truancy (*n*): the act of being absent without permission

In general, our manager isn't very **cognizant** of what goes on behind her back.

    cognizant (*adj*): fully aware

WORDS ABOUT MONEY

I took this job because my **meager** allowance just wasn't cutting it.

    meager (*adj*): very little (in quantity, substance, or size)

THE BARE NECESSITIES

RELATED WORDS

The following words all have to do with not having stuff.

Before I took this job, I was **penurious**, **impecunious**—**destitute**, even. My dad's extreme **parsimony** meant that there was no way he was going to shell out an extra twenty bucks a week for my allowance—even if I promised to be **frugal.** I was suffering from a great **paucity** of clothes, books, CDs, and concert tickets, which made me feel sad and **bereft**. Without any money, my social life was in a **derelict** condition.

> **penurious** (*adj*): lacking money or being unwilling to spend money (a rich
>   person can be penurious as well.)
> **impecunious** (*adj*): poor
> **destitute** (*adj*): desperately lacking money, food, or resources
> **parsimony** (*n*): thrift; an unwillingness to spend money
> **frugal** (*adj*): thrifty, not wasteful
> **paucity** (*n*): a lack of something
> **bereft** (*adj*): deprived of something; filled with a sense of loss
> **derelict** (*adj*): neglected and in poor condition; also, (*n*) someone who has
>   no home, employment, or family

I tried to borrow five bucks from my brothers, but they said they'd only do it if I paid them twenty dollars next week. No way am I getting involved in that kind of **usury**!

> **usury** (*n*): lending money at an extremely high rate of interest

My father said he wouldn't increase my allowance because he didn't want to support my **prodigal** ways.

> **prodigal** (*adj*): wasteful

This job isn't all that **lucrative**, but it does mean I can stop bugging my dad for money all the time.

> **lucrative** (*adj*): producing profit

THE BARE NECESSITIES

These words all have to do with making money.

I thought about taking an unpaid volunteer job this year, but I needed something that was going to be **remunerative**. I don't need to be **affluent** or anything, but my meager savings do need to be **augmented** somehow. If I can just **accrue** a little money each week—and not blow it all at once—I might just be **prosperous** at the end of the year.

remunerative (*adj*): paying or rewarding someone with money. Be careful you don't switch the *n* and the *m* in this word!

affluent (*adj*): wealthy

augment (*v*): to increase, supplement

accrue (*v*): to increase in value or amount over time

prosperous (*adj*): wealthy, successful, or fortunate. The word is similar to *affluent*, but *affluent* only deals with material wealth; *prosperous* usually implies wealth, but can also mean "successful" more generally.

YOUR TURN

In each of the groups below, choose the word that does not belong.

1. piquant   pungent   colorful   malodorous
2. impecunious   destitute   affluent   bereft
3. effortless   arduous   laborious   onerous
4. palatable   revolting   succulent   delectable

Indicate whether the pairs of words below have similar or different meanings.

5. mundane   quotidian
6. haughty   snobbish
7. prodigal   frugal
8. oleaginous   dry
9. paucity   abundance
10. augment   expand

Choose the best word from the list to fill in the blanks. Not every word will be used.

diligent corpulent unparalleled redolent dreg stultifying glutton
bereft strenuous interminable affluence abysmal coagulate malodorous epicurean fetid consumption palatable piquant

11. The house was _____ of tomato sauce after my brothers made a huge pot of pasta.
12. America is a country full of _____ people who eat too much and don't exercise.
13. I spent a(n) _____ hour in detention, staring at the wall.
14. My brothers left their _____ gym bags in the front hallway, and they soon stunk up the entire house.
15. My dad wishes my brothers and I were more _____ about our homework; he hates having slackers for kids.
16. After I blew all my money on concert tickets, I was left completely _____.

17. When I get older, I plan to marry into serious money and live a life of
    _____.

18. My father is a(n) _____ and enjoys a fine meal.

19. My brothers don't share his refined taste, but they also enjoy food—maybe
    too much. They eat so much, I'd be tempted to call them _____
    (s).

20. Wayne left a plate of leftover chicken in the fridge, and as it got more and
    more rotten, all the fat started to _____.

21. If I get to the dinner table too late, my brothers will have eaten everything,
    leaving only the _____(s) for me.

22. The F I got on my last math exam was the most _____ grade I've
    ever received.

23. Lifting barbells is _____ work.

24. High school seems _____. Sometimes I feel like I'll be stuck in it
    forever.

25. The R.E.M. concert I saw in 2000 remains a(n) _____ musical
    experience.

CHAPTER 5

HOW TO TALK ABOUT WRITING AND APPEARANCE

Essay Question No. 1: Write about a significant moment in your life and what you learned from it.

Name: Alex Lee
Prospective Class: 2005

When I was sixteen, I decided to shave my head. It wasn't a rebellion thing, and it wasn't a fashion thing. I was just tired of it, to tell you the truth. I was tired of having to push it out of my face all the time. I was tired of brushing it, and I was tired of all the shampoo I went through each month and the way I always seemed to leave a handful of it in the shower drain. I was tired of it looking all girly and windswept in photos. I thought to myself, I am not the kind of girl who should have long hair.

Problem is, I'm also not the kind of girl who should have a shaved head. All of a sudden, my ears stuck out in strange angles, and my eyebrows—which had always been hidden under a curtain of hair—seemed like huge caterpillars stretching out across my forehead. Also, I never realized it before, but there is a small, potato-shaped dent in the back of my head. Over dinner, my twin brothers took turns aiming at it with pieces of broccoli.

My father hated it. I suppose any red-blooded American father would hate to see their little princess come home with a shaved head, but my dad really took the cake. I thought he was going to cry when he saw my bald, nubby head. But then he started screaming, and I lost all sympathy for him after that. He told me I looked like a bum, instead of a young lady who had grown up with a perfectly nice family in a perfectly nice suburb of a perfectly nice city. I screamed right back

43

and told him he had a totally outdated view on women. When we visited my grandmother a few weeks later, he made me wear a San Francisco Giants hat the whole time. My grandmother wanted to know when I had gotten into football. I lied and told her I was considering a career in sports management.

My dad only loosened up when it started growing back; wispy and spiky at first, then finally into a short pageboy cut that curled over my ears. The six months in between, though, were rough. People sniggered at me in homeroom when they thought I wasn't listening. Little kids pointed at me in the mall and asked their parents what had happened to my hair. I felt really self-righteous when I was bald. Despite all this, though, I was glad when it grew back. I was tired of always having to explain it, or justify it, or fight about it. People are much nicer to me now, but whenever I look in the mirror I think about the time when I had no hair. People can be awfully rude when you don't look, act, or think the way they want you to.

And that's what I learned when I shaved my head.

* * * * *

WORDS ABOUT WRITING

I thought about beginning my essay with the line, "It was a dark and stormy night," but then I thought that sounded too **hackneyed**.

hackneyed (*adj*): stale, overused

RELATED WORDS

The following words all have to do with bad, unimaginative writing.

The sample essay my teacher gave me to read was a total nightmare. It was so **banal** and **prosaic**, it sounded like a six-year-old had written it. I mean, really— had this person ever had an original thought in her life? It was all about how volunteering at an animal shelter changed the way she thought about animals' rights. Well, duh! What a **facile** conclusion. And to make things worse, she kept peppering her essay with **trite** metaphors like "my heart sang like a bird." Yech.

banal (*adj*): boring, ordinary

prosaic (*adj*): simplistic, unsubtle, and unimaginative

facile (*adj*): made without real thought or feeling, and therefore of little value. *Facile* can also mean "requiring little effort."

trite (*adj*): overused, unoriginal

The first draft of my essay was too long and **amorphous**, so I decided to rewrite the whole thing from scratch in order to tighten it up.

amorphous (*adj*): shapeless

My tendency to **digress** meant that my essay was **diffuse** and **nebulous**: it became hard to see the point of it all. My writing was taking a **circuitous** path to its conclusion—telling stories about vacations, about our pets, and anything else that popped in my mind—and that meant that the final essay was too **convoluted** for anyone to follow.

digress (*v*): to move away from the current topic

diffuse (*adj*): spread out

nebulous (*adj*): shapeless, indistinct

circuitous (*adj*): lengthy and indirect

convoluted (*adj*): too complicated to understand easily

In my first draft, I began my essay with a story about the first haircut I ever gave myself, which seemed like a **germane** way to start things off.

germane (*adj*): appropriately related, on-topic

Okay, including a photograph of my bald head with the essay might have been a bit **superfluous**.

superfluous (*adj*): extra, unnecessary

Talking about the first haircut I ever gave my dog was, I admit, a bit **tangential**, but it was a really funny story.

tangential (*adj*): only somewhat relevant to the topic at hand

After all my editing, though, my final draft was tight and **succinct**. Every word had its place, and it didn't waste any time.

succinct (*adj*): clear, to the point

WRITING AND APPEARANCE

I had to **abridge** the part about my brothers' reaction to my haircut and **curtail** the discussion of my family's hair history in order to get my essay under the required word limit.

> **abridge** (*v*): to shorten something by cutting certain parts out
>
> **curtail** (*v*): to cut short

In order to really **elucidate** my dad's reaction, I have to tell you how he went bald at twenty-three and was very sensitive about it.

> **elucidate** (*v*): to clarify, to explain

My writing teacher suggested I write an essay about a small, domestic incident, rather than a **pretentious** essay about how I was going to save the world or write the next great American novel.

> **pretentious** (*adj*): having an unrealistically high self-image

The story of my haircut was such a **saga**—the arguments lasted for weeks.

> **saga** (*n*): a long, dramatic tale

At first I was going to write an essay about what I learned from my after-school job, but then that seemed too boring and **derivative**. Doesn't everyone write that essay?

> **derivative** (*adj*): taking ideas from somewhere else, unoriginal

Janet was away on vacation when Head Shaving '03 happened. For a while I thought about writing my essay in an **epistolary** form, and using our emails to tell the story.

> **epistolary** (*adj*): a text written in the form of letters or correspondence

WORDS ABOUT FIGHTING

My fashion choices have always **perturbed** my dad, who's pretty conservative.

> **perturb** (*v*): to trouble or worry someone

RELATED WORDS

I remember he got really **agitated** when I bought my first pair of big, leather boots. I only **exacerbated** that situation by getting my nose pierced a week later.
>   **agitate** (*v*): to make someone feel anxious or disturbed
>   **exacerbate** (*v*): to make a bad situation worse

The head-shaving incident caused **discord** in my house: My father kept yelling and then refused to talk to me.
>   **discord** (*n*): disagreement and strife; or, what results when harsh sounds clash with one another, making an unpleasant noise

My dad has always claimed to be a free thinker and really easygoing, which meant that his off-the-wall behavior that day was quite **dissonant**.
>   **dissonant** (*n*): inconsistent, incompatible. In musical terms, it means making a harsh, unpleasant sound by combining particular notes.

My dad **castigated** me by grounding me for two weeks.
>   **castigate** (*v*): to criticize or punish someone severely

I can't believe it—my brothers break a family heirloom vase and only get **reprimanded**. I shave my head—my own head, thank you!—and I get two weeks with no TV, no phone, and no social life.
>   **reprimand** (*v*): to rebuke someone; less harsh than *castigate*

I told my dad he would **acclimate** to my new hair, but he seemed really doubtful.
>   **acclimate** (*v*): to get used to

He was **adamant** that I buy a wig for the upcoming class pictures.
>   **adamant** (*v*): firm, unyielding

He **scoffed** when I told him that plenty of famous models had shaved heads now.
>   **scoff** (*v*): to mock or scorn

The whole situation got us both really **disgruntled**.
>   **disgruntled** (*adj*): upset

He tried to **dissuade** me from keeping it bald until prom.
>   **dissuade** (*v*): to persuade someone not to do something

The event was quite **divisive** in my house. My brothers felt torn, because they didn't know whom to side with.
>   **divisive** (*adj*): causing disagreement and hostility

WRITING AND APPEARANCE

WORDS ABOUT APPEARANCE

I liked my new rebel haircut. I practiced an angry, punk-rock **countenance** to go along with it.

> **countenance** (*n*): facial expression

My dad thought a shaved head wasn't **seemly** for a young lady.

> **seemly** (*adj*): proper, pleasant-looking

RELATED WORDS

I told him I wasn't interested in being that kind of **decorous**, proper girl.

> **decorous** (*adj*): well-mannered, dignified

My father still **adheres** to some old-fashioned, antiquated sense of appropriateness.

> **adhere** (*v*): to stick to something firmly

My dad is really **fastidious** about his own appearance. Every morning, he spends fifteen minutes making sure his sideburns, moustache, and nose hairs are all perfectly trimmed.

> **fastidious** (*adj*): fussy, concerned with details, very clean

I told him he was being **superficial**—shouldn't he be more concerned with the fact that I am a good person?

> **superficial** (*adj*): overly concerned with appearances and surfaces, shallow

I think that, in parent-child relations, looks should be **inconsequential**. What if I had been born really ugly?

> **inconsequential** (*adj*): not important

Janet told me my new 'do **accentuated** my eyes.

> **accentuate** (*v*): to emphasize or draw attention to a particular feature

I told my dad that I liked being **eccentric**. Who wants to look like everyone else? Or worse—like a fashion spread in *Seventeen*?

> **eccentric** (*adj*): unconventional

My dad said there was a difference between being eccentric and being **aberrant**.
   aberrant (*adj*): abnormal, deviant. It's a much stronger word than *eccentric*.

It wasn't like someone had **defaced** his property. It's my head, and besides—I liked the way it looked.
   deface (*v*): to ruin the appearance of something

He acted as if I had been **defiled**. Good Lord, Dad, it's just a haircut! I'm still the same girl I was yesterday.
   defile (*v*): to dirty something

He thought it made me look like a girl of **disrepute** (in other words, a girl who wouldn't get into an Ivy League school).
   disrepute (*n*): a bad reputation

He said I looked like a **wastrel** and a punk. I told him he looked like he had a stick shoved up his backside, but he wasn't going to hear me complaining.
   wastrel (*n*): an offensive term for someone who is lazy and wasteful

Personally, I think I have great **sartorial** taste.
   sartorial (*adj*): relating to clothing

YOUR TURN

Indicate whether the pairs of words below have similar or different meanings.

1. diffuse   succinct
2. perturb   soothe
3. aberrant   eccentric
4. elucidate   explain
5. disgruntled   satisfied
6. convoluted   circuitous
7. superficial   shallow
8. hackneyed   banal
9. abridge   curtail
10. reprimand   praise

Choose the word that best completes the sentence.

11. Lots of people complain about violence on TV, which is usually
    _____ and doesn't contribute anything to the actual program.
    (A) trite (B) amorphous (C) superfluous (D) convoluted

12. My brothers like to _____ me when I'm trying to concentrate on,
    say, writing a new poem.
    (A) castigate (B) deface (C) acclimate (D) agitate

13. When you go to a museum, you have to behave _____: no running
    around or yelling in the halls.
    (A) decorously (B) aberrantly (C) nebulously (D) tangentially

14. When my dad got a one-hundred-dollar telephone bill last month, he had
    to _____ our phone usage.
    (A) adhere (B) elucidate (C) defile (D) curtail

15. When I failed that last math test, Janet tried to comfort me by saying it was a really _____ test and wouldn't affect my grade too much.
(A) germane (B) tangential (C) inconsequential (D) divisive

16. Walter Chen is incredibly _____. He's always acting like he's better and smarter than everyone else, but he's totally not.
(A) pretentious (B) prosaic (C) convoluted (D) disgruntled

17. My brothers and I like really loud rock music, but my dad says it all just sounds like _____ to him.
(A) wastrel (B) dissonance (C) saga (D) reprimands

18. Janet and I wanted to take the scenic route, so we drove on a _____ path and took two hours longer than necessary.
(A) disreputable (B) adamant (C) accentuated (D) circuitous

19. My dad thinks my big, clunky combat boots aren't _____ for a young lady.
(A) seemly (B) derivative (C) superfluous (D) tangential

20. It took me a while to _____ to high school; the whole place didn't make sense to me at first.
(A) curtail (B) acclimate (C) exacerbate (D) scoff

21. Our teacher really liked Walter's short story, even though it was totally _____ of a story we had read last year.
(A) decorous (B) defaced (C) derivative (D) agitated

22. The noise of the construction across the street _____ my already terrible headache.
(A) exacerbated (B) elucidated (C) digressed (D) defiled

23. The book *Griffin and Sabine* is a(n) _____ novel—it's written as a series of letters and postcards.
(A) divisive (B) discordant (C) epistolary (D) abridged

24. Last night I had a really scary nightmare, but when I woke up I had only a(n) _____ memory of what happened in it.
    (A) trite (B) nebulous (C) circuitous (D) pretentious

25. My father is _____ about my going to college next year.
    (A) adamant (B) discordant (C) fastidious (D) succinct

CHAPTER 6

HOMONYMS

So, my brothers found out I was doing this book and got really upset that they weren't being included. After much haggling, I agreed to give them two chapters in exchange for their doing the dishes for a week. Here goes—I take no responsibility for this one!

*   *   *   *   *

Hey, so we're Alex's brothers. First of all, don't listen to anything she says about us! It's all lies! She'd like you to believe that we're the troublemakers in the house, but everyone knows that *she's* the criminal mastermind, and we're just the poor suckers who get blamed for everything.

This is so cool. We have our own chapter in a book! This is wicked. Think of all the people who are reading these very words *right now* . . . . Ah, think of the power!

But, um . . . now that we have this chapter . . . we don't know what to do with it. This whole thing was way cooler in theory. Crap—now it's like homework!

Well, we suppose we could tell you a story. But all our good stories involve activities that are illegal in most states. And frankly, it would be pretty stupid for us to put those here in print. But I'm sure, if we think about it for a while, we can think of something to keep you entertained.

Oh, okay. Here's one. Once, we went to Great America, which is this massive theme park in northern California. Mike stood in line to get on the skyline tram ride—you know, one of those slow rides that takes you across the whole park in about twenty minutes. While he's in line he starts hassling the ride attendant, asking him all kinds of questions about how safe the ride is. He asks when it was last tested, and how many fatalities there have been since it was installed. The guy assured Mike that there was no danger. "What if the wind is, like, blowing really, really hard?" Mike asked. "Could I get blown out of the car?" The guy is getting totally pissed at Mike, and all these little kids behind him are complaining because they want to get on the ride. Finally, the attendant is all, "Look kid, if you don't want to get on the ride, just get out of line." Mike made a big show of looking scared, but then climbed into the little car. He buckled his safety belt, took several deep showy breaths, and gripped the railing as the car took off.

Meanwhile, Wayne had been waiting around the corner, dressed in exactly the same outfit, but covered in dirt and all these fake bruises. After about ten minutes—when there was *no* chance Mike could have gotten off the ride, Wayne went up to the ride attendant and started yelling stuff like, "You jackass! You told me this ride was safe!" The guy was so freaked out he gave Wayne all these free food coupons. Wayne took down the attendant's name and information and stormed off, leaving all these little kids screaming their heads off in line.

It was amazing. And we each got a free pizza out of it!

* * * * *

Sigh. Alex again. Sorry about that! But my stupid brothers did give me a good vocabulary idea. People are always confusing Mike and Wayne because they look exactly alike. There are also a lot of "twinned" words out there that always get mixed up. These words are called **homophones** (words that are pronounced the same way but have different meanings) or **homographs** (words that are spelled the same way but have different meanings). These two categories of words, when taken together, are called *homonyms*. Think of pairs like "hare" (the animal) and "hair" (which grows on your head), or "lead" (the metal) and "lead" (to walk ahead of someone).

* * * * *

The following words are pairs that are always confused. Keep 'em straight and you'll be way ahead of the pack (but that's no guarantee you'll be safe from Mike and Wayne!).

HOMONYMS

Even though my brothers are completely identical, they're still two **discrete** human beings. Still, the similarity is pretty uncanny. Little kids (who are not known for being **discreet**) often point and stare at them in public.

discrete (*adj*): separate, unconnected
discreet (*adj*): modest, cautious

Since they were eleven, my brothers' growth has been **continuous**. They seem to grow an inch and a half every year. My father is **continually** having to buy them new pants and shoes.

    continuous (*adj*): going on without change or interruption
    continual (*adj*): happening again and again

A girl once convinced Wayne to take a dance class. Problem is, he has no rhythm. He **foundered** pretty miserably—though I, for one, enjoyed watching him **flounder** around, trying to find the beat.

    founder (*v*): to collapse, to fail (literally, it means to sink under water)
    flounder (*v*): to move about clumsily

Mike had to write an essay for English class on an **abstract** concept (like love, honor, tradition, etc.) He sat **abstracted** at his desk for a long time, staring out the window and trying to come up with a topic.

    abstract (*adj*): something that can't be touched or held, but can only be
        understood intellectually
    abstracted (*adj*): deep in thought

When Wayne decided to **abjure** red meat, he **adjured** Mike to do likewise.

    abjure (*v*): to reject or avoid something
    adjure (*v*): to order someone to do something

After my brothers **arrogated** the car for a late-night joyride, Dad **abrogated** their Internet usage for a whole month.

    arrogate (*v*): to take or claim something without the right to do so
    abrogate (*v*): to cancel, to repeal

Mike and Wayne want to open a veterinary clinic someday. Mike will **administer** the organization while Wayne **ministers** to the animals.

    administer (*v*): to manage the business affairs of a person or organization
    minister (*v*): to care for someone's needs

Mike and Wayne are **averse** to doing their homework, because looking "like a coupla nerds" would be **adverse** to their popularity.

    averse (*adj*): strongly disliking something
    adverse (*adj*): harmful, unfavorable

Ever since they saw *The Matrix*, Mike and Wayne are constantly making **allusions** to that movie. Whenever they have to make a tough decision, they refer to it as choosing between "the red pill or the blue pill." They love the idea that the world as they know it is just an **illusion**. I told them that even if it were true, they wouldn't be any cooler in the real world.

> **allusion** (*n*): a reference to an event, person, piece of literature, etc., that doesn't explicitly identify what that thing or person is
> **illusion** (*n*): a deceptive vision, a hallucination

When trying to **elude** being punished by our dad, Mike and Wayne often try to argue their way out by **alluding** to Dad's own stupid, youthful behavior.

> **elude** (*v*): to avoid, to escape
> **allude** (*v*): to make an **allusion** (see above)

Mike has big **calluses** on his feet, and Wayne is always **callously** making fun of him for it.

> **callus** (*n*): a buildup of hard skin, as on the fingers of a guitar player
> **callous** (*adj*): cold, unfeeling

When the school administration tried to **censor** *The Catcher in the Rye*, I wrote an editorial **censuring** the decision.

> **censor** (*v*): to remove or edit something because of offensive content
> **censure** (*v*): to criticize severely

Mike and Wayne once tried to write a screenplay. It was a thriller about **climatic** researchers, and the **climactic** moment involved a series of killer tornadoes.

> **climatic** (*adj*): having to do with the weather
> **climactic** (*adj*): describing the most exciting, important moment in a movie, story, novel, etc.

When I shaved my head, my brothers **complimented** me on the fact that my new 'do now **complemented** my sullen, nonconformist attitude.

> **compliment** (*v*): a flattering comment
> **complement** (*adj*): to go well with something; to complete

Mike and Wayne accepted the **counsel** of the student **council** and ran a car wash to raise money for the soccer team.

> **counsel** (*n*): advice
> **council** (*n*): a group of people working in an official capacity

When my father **descried** the girlie mags hidden under my brothers' beds, he **decried** Mike and Wayne for having brought them into the house.

> **descry** (v): to discover something
> **decry** (v): to strongly criticize

When they were eleven and dorky, they wanted to write a **definitive** guide to Magic: The Gathering. Now that they're fifteen and popular, bringing that up as often as possible is a **definite** way for me to embarrass them.

> **definitive** (adj): the ultimate, most authoritative example or edition of something
> **definite** (adj): sure, unquestionable

Mike and Wayne have really self-**deprecating** senses of humor. They're always making fun of themselves, yet it doesn't seem to cause their popularity to **depreciate** at all—in fact, I think people like them more for it.

> **deprecate** (v): to put down
> **depreciate** (v): to go down in value

Mike and Wayne **disassembled** the computer in one day. When they couldn't put it back together, they **dissembled** and told Dad I had done it.

> **disassemble** (v): to take apart
> **dissemble** (v): to lie, to pretend

My father is always trying to **elicit** information from me about my brothers' **illicit** activities.

> **elicit** (v): to draw information out
> **illicit** (adj): illegal

When the huge flu **epidemic** was sweeping through our high school, Mike and Wayne—with their **endemic** good luck—managed to avoid catching anything.

> **epidemic** (n): wide-spreading phenomenon (usually an unfavorable one)
> **endemic** (adj): characteristic

Dad gives each of us kids an **equable** amount of money for allowance. But I don't think it's **equitable** that I get the same twenty dollars a week my brothers get—after all, I'm three years older than they are!

> **equable** (adj): even, unchanging
> **equitable** (adj): fair, just

Rather than ask Dad for money to buy concert tickets, Mike and Wayne decided it would be more **expedient** to "borrow" it from his wallet. Dad found out, though, and gave them the nasty task of cleaning out the garage. No matter how **expeditiously** they worked, there was no way they were going to finish that job in less than three months.

> **expedient** (*adj*): practical, suitable for a particular purpose
> **expeditious** (*adj*): done quickly and efficiently

Once, my brothers tried to **ferment** their own wine in our basement. I told Dad about it, and they blamed me for **fomenting** dissent in the house.

> **ferment** (*v*): to undergo or cause to undergo a biochemical process that breaks substances down into simpler ones (alcohol, for example, is created by *fermenting* sugar)
> **foment** (*v*): to stir up, to incite (usually trouble, revolution, or other disruptive things)

Wayne's claim that he wrote that brilliant paper about the **fictional** character Othello is totally **fictitious**—I know for a fact he got it off the Internet.

> **fictional** (*adj*): drawn from a work of fiction
> **fictitious** (*adj*): a lie, not true

YOUR TURN

Match the vocab words on the left with their definitions on the right.

1.	climactic	a.	a biochemical process
2.	climatic	b.	to reject
3.	decry	c.	a patch of hardened skin
4.	descry	d.	advice
5.	allusion	e.	to command
6.	illusion	f.	a false vision
7.	abjure	g.	a plague
8.	adjure	h.	to criticize
9.	callous	i.	a group working on official matters
10.	callus	j.	hard-hearted
11.	council	k.	to discover
12.	counsel	l.	a reference to a person or thing
13.	endemic	m.	having to do with the weather
14.	epidemic	n.	to provoke trouble
15.	ferment	o.	typical, distinctive
16.	foment	p.	exciting, decisive

Choose the best word from the list given below to fill in the blanks. Not every word will be used.

compliment   complement   equitable   equable   dissemble   disassemble
definitive   definite   elude   allude   censure   censor   abrogate   arrogate
continual   continuous

17. Yesterday, Mike actually paid me a _____. He said I didn't look as awful as I normally do.

18. The editor spent twenty-eight years preparing the _____ edition of *Hamlet*.

19. When I was little, my parents would often _____ me for bullying my brothers.

20. At MFC, the division of labor isn't _____. I always seem to be working so much harder than anyone else.

21. My brothers often _____ in order to get out of chores. They pretend they're going to the library, and then they go play video games at their friend's house.

22. Our principal, Mr. Limbergh, keeps threatening to _____ our off-campus lunch privileges.

23. The escaped convict managed to _____ capture for a full six months.

24. I thought the orange couch would _____ my purple carpet nicely, but Janet disagreed.

25. When my brothers got the new Limp Bizkit album, they played it _____ly for a week with no break.

CHAPTER 7
HOW TO TALK ABOUT MUSIC AND CONCERTS

By nine o' clock, the Tin Cup was wall-to-wall packed with a solid Friday crowd. The floor was sticky with spilled drinks, and the air was thick with excitement. I spent most of the time fixing my stupid tube top, cursing Janet the whole time for convincing me to wear "something hot." We saw Walter lurking in the corner, and we waved—we thought it was probably a good idea to stay in his good graces. He was talking to Tom the DJ, who also spun at the poetry nights. Tom kept looking around for someone to save him.

The folks at the Cup had put together a good, varied show. Janet's favorite was this alt-country band, Rose's Turn, which featured three fiddles, a banjo, and a harmonica. Then there was a skate punk band (which I hated) and a fake metal band called Kingdom of the Blind (which I loved), and what seemed like a million bands in between. Finally, around midnight, they announced that Rex's band, the Giants, was up. The postcard Walter had handed me said they were a "lo-fi indie garage extravaganza." I wasn't really sure what that meant, but it sounded good to me.

And they sounded even better once they got on stage. A loud, raw set that clocked under twenty minutes—now *that's* the way rock and roll should be! Janet and I spent the entire time jumping around and dancing up a sweat in the first row. I tried desperately not to stare at Rex, who had the whole yeah-I'm-in-this-awesome-band-but-it's-no-big-deal pose down cold. And not only did he look good up there, but he was one of the best guitar players I'd ever heard—and I'm a really harsh critic. When he started to sing I was amazed at what a sweet voice he had. I mean, the guy could've been a choirboy; it was completely adorable. I spent the entire time staring at his shoes, worried that if I caught his eyes I'd faint and get trampled by all the pogo-ing high schoolers.

Janet ran off to the bathroom during their last song, but I kept dancing by myself. When the set was over, I stuck around by the stage, hoping to figure out a way to score an introduction. Lucky for me, Walter had started talking to Rex. Perfect opportunity, I thought, as I made my way over to them. "Hey," I said, trying to sound all cool and sultry. "That was a fantastic set. You guys are very . . ." and then I took a long pause, as if I hadn't planned out the whole line in advance. "Very Sonic Youth meets the Velvet Underground, with a little bit of the Strokes," I finished triumphantly.

The boys were quiet for a second. Wow, I thought. That must have really floored them. Go ahead and try to tell *me* that girls don't know anything about rock music. Who's your daddy *now*? "Um, thanks," Rex said finally. Walter had a dazed look on his face, and when I tried to see what he was looking at . . . I realized that, as I was moshing, I had somehow managed to spring free from my tube top. Losing all pretense of cool, I started trying to stuff myself back in my shirt when Janet came out of the bathroom. Thinking fast, she swooped in and grabbed me, making some excuse about curfew as she pulled me out the door. Thankfully, she managed to get out to the parking lot before bursting into uncontrollable laughter.

"Smooth move, Ex-Lax!" she guffawed, completely ignoring the death stares I was shooting at her.

"I'm going to kill you, Gonzales," I muttered. "Just drive me home already!"

*   *   *   *   *

WORDS ABOUT MUSIC

The punk band let loose with a lot of **cacophonous** noise. Thank God I brought my earplugs.

cacophonous (*adj*): harsh-sounding, unpleasantly loud

RELATED WORDS

The following words describe sounds.

The crowd was **clamorous**, clapping and yelling for all the bands and making a huge, **vociferous** noise.

    clamorous (*adj*): making a loud, insistent noise

    vociferous (*adj*): characterized by loud shouting

The first band used a cello, which added a **mellifluous** element to its more traditional guitar and drums.

    mellifluous (*adj*): pleasant, rich in tone

The singer had a **dulcet** voice—almost out of place here at a rock show.

    dulcet (*adj*): pleasant, soft, and soothing

I wish I had a voice as **sultry** as hers. I bet guys line up to get her number after shows.

    sultry (*adj*): low-pitched and sexy (usually applied to a woman)

The bass player joined her for a few songs, adding his deep, **sonorous** baritone voice to her sweeter, higher one.

    sonorous (*adj*): deep, resonant

One band had eight instruments and sounded positively **symphonic**. You could tell they were all highly trained musicians.

    symphonic (*adj*): harmonious

The first singer was so nervous that her voice was barely **audible.**

    audible (*adj*): able to be heard

Rex turned out to be a **virtuoso** on the guitar.

    virtuoso (*n*): a masterful musician

I mean, I knew he was cute, but I had no idea he was such a **maestro** as well.

    maestro (*n*): an expert in a particular art, especially music

I love to hear the **convergence** of really good instrumentalists.

    convergence (*n*): coming together

At the end of their last song, Rex's band launched into a crazy **improvisation**. It was a little too Phish for me, but I was impressed anyway.

    improvisation (*n*): the performance of something that hasn't been planned beforehand

Rex's greatest **opus** was a song dedicated to his childhood skateboard.

    opus (*n*): a creative piece of work in the arts

MUSIC AND CONCERTS

Most of the bands alternated louder, harder songs with softer **ballads**.
   ballad (*n*): a slow, romantic song

Rex looked so majestic on stage, I could imagine him as a **bard** from a time long ago. Then I stopped being a moron and started listening to the show again.
   bard (*n*): a poet, particularly one of national importance

Rex had a beautiful speaking voice too. He spoke in rich **cadences** that seemed out of place at a place like the Cup.
   cadence (*n*): the way the voice rises and falls in pitch while someone is talking; the way poetry or prose flows

WORDS ABOUT PERFORMANCES AND CROWDS

After the first three bands played, I needed a **respite**. It was so hot that I left to take a walk outside for a while.
   respite (*n*): a brief rest

RELATED WORDS

When Rex's band came onstage, Rex announced that their keyboardist was on **hiatus** for a few months, but he'd be back in time for the spring Battle of the Bands.
   hiatus (*n*): a break in something where there should be continuity

With his dark good looks and his fantastic guitar skills, Rex was an **arresting** stage presence.
   arresting (*adj*): catching people's attention

Rex had an especially powerful effect on the girls in the audience—some of them looked positively **stupefied** when he started to sing. (Okay, so maybe I was one of them . . . but I caught myself, eventually, and managed to close my mouth.)
   stupefy (*v*): to amaze

Between sets, while the stage crew was setting up the next band's equipment, people tended to **dissipate** from the stage.

dissipate (*v*): to spread out

The lead singer of the punk band screeched like a **feral** animal.

feral (*adj*): like a wild animal

I'd never seen such a **congregation** of mullet-wearing hipsters in my life.

congregation (*n*): gathering of people

The singer was such a magnetic presence; if he cleaned up and made a habit of kissing babies, I could see him as a really effective **demagogue**.

demagogue (*n*): a political leader who appeals to people's emotions as opposed to their rationality

After finishing his set, the lead singer of the punk band **impudently** threw a speaker into the audience.

impudently (*adv*): done in a bold, shameless way

Synonyms for *impudently* are **brazenly** (*adv*) and **audaciously** (*adv*), which both mean fearlessly or shamelessly.

The crowd was **boisterous** tonight—they kept yelling and clapping, even during the slow songs.

boisterous (*adj*): energetic, rowdy

Some of the more **bourgeois** concertgoers seemed offended by the more explicit lyrics. What were they expecting at a rock show?

bourgeois (*adj*): behaving in a way considered typical of the affluent middle class: being materialistic, being conventional in taste and outlook

One guy sang a song of such **candor** about an ex-girlfriend that it made me a little uncomfortable. What if someone she knew was in the audience?

candor (*n*): extreme honesty

WORDS ABOUT REX

When I told Rex I liked his set, he responded with a **cryptic** "Huh." What am I supposed to make of that???
> **cryptic** (*adj*): mysterious

RELATED WORDS

I always find an **enigma** so exciting.
> **enigma** (*n*): a mystery

My feelings about Rex are far from **ambivalent**.
> **ambivalent** (*adj*): not caring one way or the other, or having mixed feelings

He seems pretty **impervious**, though. How am I ever going to get to know him?
> **impervious** (*adj*): unable to be gotten through

Rex is a **laconic** guy. Who doesn't love the strong-and-silent type?
> **laconic** (*adj*): using only a few words

Rex doesn't say more than he needs to, but he never seems **terse**; he manages to be warm without ever saying much. I can't tell if he's **reticent** because I'm weird, or if he's just **bashful**.
> **terse** (*adj*): speaking very little. A stronger word than *laconic*: implies harshness and brusqueness
> **reticent** (*adj*): unwilling to communicate
> **bashful** (*adj*): shy

Rex likes to wear a beat-up black leather jacket, and sometimes he rides a motorcycle. I swear I'd never buy into that whole **renegade** thing, but I have to admit, it does have its charms.
> **renegade** (*n*): an individual who breaks away from a group

Rex has a big scar above his eyebrow that I find particularly **alluring**.
> **alluring** (*adj*): very attractive, tempting

I can't believe I've been so easily **beguiled** by a boy . . . let alone a boy in a band. Whenever I see him, I'm so **mesmerized** I can barely form sentences. He really is pretty **sublime**. At the very least, I don't find him **repulsive**, like I do most boys my age.

> **beguile** (*v*): to charm, to seduce
> **mesmerize** (*v*): to fascinate, to hypnotize
> **sublime** (*adj*): divine, perfect
> **repulsive** (*adj*): disgusting

Rex is the **archetypal** hip, moody rock-type a girl like me is supposed to fall for. Predictably, I totally fell for him!

> **archetypal** (*adj*): providing a perfect example of something

Janet likes big football player guys, but I prefer more **lissome** boys.

> **lissome** (*adj*): slender and graceful

Janet claims I only like **emaciated** boys, because they make me feel better about how skinny I am. I say I just prefer them **sinewy**.

> **emaciated** (*adj*): overly skinny, underfed. This is a much more extreme term than *skinny*, *lissome*, or *sinewy*.
> **sinewy** (*adj*): lean but strong

Rex has this way of blinking really **languidly** before he speaks that makes my ears go all red.

> **languidly** (*adv*): sleepily moving or talking

The **antonym**, or opposite, of languidly is **animated** (*adj*): energetic, full of activity.

Rex doesn't have a **blemish** on him—he's absolutely perfect. Not that I'm obsessing or anything.

> **blemish** (*n*): a small flaw; a pimple

MUSIC AND CONCERTS

YOUR TURN

Match the vocab words on the left with the word or phrase that means the opposite on the right.

1.	animated	a.	earthly, ordinary
2.	cryptic	b.	dishonesty
3.	cacophonous	c.	straightforward
4.	ambivalent	d.	harsh, unpleasant
5.	emaciated	e.	decisive
6.	laconic	f.	attractive
7.	repulsive	g.	lifeless
8.	candor	h.	fat
9.	dulcet	i.	talkative
10.	sublime	j.	sweet sounding

In each of the groups below, choose the word that does not belong.

11. vociferous   cacophonous   sonorous   impervious

12. hiatus   respite   congregation   intermission

13. sinewy   bashful   emaciated   lissome

14. mellifluous   terse   laconic   reticent

15. alluring   symphonic   beguiling   arresting

Choose the word that best completes the sentence.

16. Yo-Yo Ma is a cello _____ who spent years studying his instrument.

    (A) bard (B) archetype (C) maestro (D) opus

17. Rock musicians like to shock their _____ audience members.

    (A) bourgeois (B) brazen (C) emaciated (D) enigmatic

18. My new raincoat is _____ to water.

    (A) reticent (B) mellifluous (C) sonorous (D) impervious

MUSIC AND CONCERTS

19. The little kids at the circus were jumping around _____ and giving me a headache.

    (A) arrestingly (B) boisterously (C) beguilingly (D) audibly

20. When the acrobats came out, though, the kids were _____ by the sight and grew very quiet.

    (A) mesmerized (B) animated (C) repulsed (D) dissipated

21. Michelangelo's "David" is the most perfect piece of art I've ever seen—there isn't a single _____ on it.

    (A) renegade (B) demagogue (C) clamor (D) blemish

22. "David" is a(n) _____ artistic masterpiece—it will be mentioned in any art history book.

    (A) mellifluous (B) enigmatic (C) archetypal (D) feral

23. I watched as the steam from my coffee slowly _____ into the air.

    (A) clamored (B) dissipated (C) stupefied (D) beguiled

24. I hate reading *Vogue* and being faced with all those _____ models. Eat something already!

    (A) emaciated (B) bashful (C) cacophonous (D) sublime

25. Rex is such an _____. I wish I could get just a tiny glimpse into the way his mind works.

    (A) ballad (B) respite (C) renegade (D) enigma

CHAPTER 8
HOW TO TALK ABOUT BRAINS

The next week, the memory of that awful moment at the Cup was still playing on constant repeat. I couldn't believe I'd made such an ass of myself. I was completely sure I would never, ever live it down. I even found myself drifting off in Ms. Lieberman's English class—something I never, ever do. English has always been my favorite subject, and the only one I've always done really well in. And Ms. Lieberman is an awesome teacher. She's really young and hip, and probably the only person on the faculty who actually believes her students have intelligent things to say. But today, even she couldn't keep me focused on *Hamlet*.

We were discussing the question of whether or not Hamlet is a hero. (Or, rather, the rest of the class was discussing that—I was doodling tiny pictures of tube tops all over my notebook.) Walter was, as usual, blabbing on about something. Sometimes it's fun to watch Walter get all worked up; I keep expecting his head to turn into a steam whistle, like in cartoons. But I hate people who argue just for the sake of arguing, which it sounded like Walter was doing now.

"I mean, he's just really *lame*," Walter was saying, his voice getting higher and louder with each word. "He has no direction and he can't make up his mind about anything. He's so wishy-washy it drives me crazy. Determination—*that's* what makes a person successful." He said it as if he'd just made the most brilliant observation ever.

The self-righteous tone in Walter's voice was too much for me to take. "Oh, come off it, Walter. Hamlet's not wishy-washy. He's just gone through a *lot*. I mean, his dad was killed, his mom married his dad's murderer, he's being haunted, and everyone's out to get him. Shakespeare wrote the character as a normal guy with problems—he's not supposed to be Superman."

Walter narrowed his eyes at me. "Just because *you* go in for tortured artist-types doesn't mean *all* of us do, Lee."

A couple people sniggered. Once again, I wanted to smack Walter into the next time zone. Or, at least, I would have wanted to do that, if I hadn't been so surprised that he'd sussed out my crush.

"Okay, guys, okay, simmer down," Ms. Lieberman said, eyeing the two of us. Just then the bell rang, and everyone cleared out before she could yell out the assignment.

"You didn't need to get all *snippy* with me, you know," said Walter as he put his books away.

"Yeah, well, Walter, I suppose I'm feeling a lot like Hamlet these days," I said as I threw on my backpack. "I mean, *you* may have it all figured out, Mr. Princeton, but that doesn't mean the *rest* of us do." And with that I clomped on out of class.

Great. That reminds me. I've got a college interview coming up. This week just keeps getting better and better. . . .

*   *   *   *   *

WORDS ABOUT WALTER

Nothing but **acrimonious** words passes between Walter Chen and me.
    acrimonious (*adj*): bitter, hateful

RELATED WORDS

We used to be friendly in the fourth grade, when we were in the same carpool. But now there is only **rancor**, **acerbity**, and **spite** between us. He can't even pass me a pencil without shooting me **inimical** looks and muttering **virulently** under his breath.
    rancor (*n*): hatred, bitterness
    acerbity (*n*): bitterness in tone or manner
    spite (*n*): a small-minded desire to hurt someone
    inimical (*adj*): hostile
    virulently (*adv*): poisonously, bitterly

Whenever I look at him, I can see all kinds of **nefarious** plots being plotted in his brain.

   nefarious (*adj*): wicked

A synonym for *nefarious* is **pernicious** (*adj*): destructive, wicked.

I think the rest of the class was a little taken aback by the **asperity** in our voices.

   asperity (*n*): harshness, severity

Janet thinks the way that Walter and I fight is pretty **despicable**—especially since she suspects Walter is still harboring a crush on me that dates back to middle school.

   despicable (*adj*): contemptible

After our encounter in class, I was really tempted to write some really **injurious** things about him on the stalls of the girls' room.

   injurious (*adj*): hurtful

A synonym for *injurious* is **deleterious** (*adj*): harmful.

He really is a nasty little **miscreant**.

   miscreant (*n*): villain; contemptible person

WORDS ABOUT INTELLECT AND EDUCATION

Our English teacher, Ms. Lieberman, is incredibly **erudite**—she's got more degrees than a thermometer.

   erudite (*adj*): highly learned

BRAINS

RELATED WORDS

She's not only book-smart, she's also really **savvy** when it comes to people. She's very **perspicacious** about human behavior, and has an **acute** sense of how to handle teenagers. I wish some of the more **obtuse** teachers at this school would take a clue from her.

> **savvy** (*adj*): shrewd, well-informed
> **perspicacious** (*adj*): perceptive, discerning
> **acute** (*adj*): sharp, smart
> **obtuse** (*adj*): dull, stupid

Acute and *obtuse* are direct antonyms. They're taken from geometry—an *acute* angle is less than 90°, and an *obtuse* angle is greater than 90° (which means an *acute* angle is, literally, sharp).

She's really patient—she once took an entire class period to walk us through a particularly **intricate** poem that we were having trouble understanding.

> **intricate** (*adj*): complicated, with many small parts

I feel bad about a really **execrable** paper I wrote on Conrad's *Heart of Darkness* this semester.

> **execrable** (*adj*): very low-quality

She's never **didactic**; she'll tell you what she thinks about the book, but she's always willing to listen to one of our crazy hypotheses.

> **didactic** (*adj*): instructional, especially in a way that's overly preachy

I appreciate the fact that she's open to all our suggestions—unlike some teachers, who are total **doctrinaires** when it comes to running his or her classrooms.

> **doctrinaire** (*n*): someone who refuses to consider other theories or approaches besides their own

I way prefer Ms. Lieberman's **pedagogy** over my former English teachers', which seemed to consist of mainly boring vocab quizzes, dry lectures, and patronizing assignments.

> **pedagogy** (*n*): the science of teaching

I imagine Ms. Lieberman spends her free time reading hoity-toity literary journals and sipping tea with other members of the **intelligentsia**.

> **intelligentsia** (*n*): the most educated members of a society

Because I respect her so much, I try to be really **deliberate** in all my work for her class.

    deliberate (*adj*): careful, methodical

WORDS ABOUT ARGUING

Walter and I get so mad at each other, our arguments sometimes **degenerate** into plain shouting matches.

    degenerate (*v*): to become worse

When he gets excited about something, Walter's voice goes all high-pitched and **abrasive**.

    abrasive (*adj*): grating, insensitive

Sometimes Janet begs me to just **acquiesce** to Walter and save everyone else the misery of hearing us argue.

    acquiesce (*v*): to agree passively

I think, however, that he needs to be exposed as the intellectual **charlatan** he is.

    charlatan (*n*): fraud, imposter

Seriously, I've never met anyone more **disputatious** than Walter. If you mention that it's a beautiful day outside, he'll find a way to argue that it's actually cloudy.

    disputatious (*adj*): argumentative

RELATED WORDS

Contentious (*adj*) and **pugnacious** (*adj*) are synonyms for *disputatious*.

    Here are some other words about arguing.

I'll never forget the day Walter **remonstrated** with me for a whole hour about how public school students should all be forced to wear uniforms. Later that day he emailed me a whole **polemic** on the subject.

    remonstrate (*v*): to argue forcefully
    polemic (*n*): a passionately worded argument

BRAINS

I try not to **disparage** Walter on a regular basis, but it's hard.

disparage (*v*): to put down

Once I managed to **discredit** Walter in class by pointing out that he'd stolen his entire argument about Bush's foreign policy from the *New York Times* editorial that morning. Walter **disdains** unoriginal thinkers, so it was a particularly good hit for me. I wasn't surprised to hear later that he'd been **maligning** me to the rest of the chess team.

discredit (*v*): to cast doubt on something

disdain (*v*): to have contempt for

malign (*v*): to say or write bad things about someone

I even emailed him the editorial later as **incontrovertible** proof.

incontrovertible (*adj*): unable to be denied

Walter should try to be more **obdurate**—he's too easily swayed by teasing.

obdurate (*adj*): not easily moved by pity or emotion

When he gets going, though, he's totally **intractable**. I really get a kick out of fighting with him; you never know what he's going to throw at you.

intractable (*adj*): difficult to manage or deal with

Whenever Walter starts a fight, I find it hard to **demur**.

demur (*v*): to object mildly

I find it kind of honorable how Walter will stick with a line of argumentation, even if it's totally **untenable**.

untenable (*adj*): unsupportable

Walter doesn't say much unless he's fighting, and then he's positively **voluble**.

voluble (*adj*): talkative

Sometimes I want to **concur** with his arguments, but I'd never give him the satisfaction.

concur (*v*): to agree

I often have to **suppress** the urge to punch Walter in the nose when I pass him in the halls.

suppress (*v*): to resist certain thoughts as they arise

BRAINS

Sometimes I find his smugness and self-confidence irritatingly **presumptuous**—who does he think he is?

> **presumptuous** (*adj*): overconfident, especially when not entitled to be doing something

Ms. Lieberman always says that, if Walter and I could ever stop arguing long enough to join our energies and **collaborate**, we'd be an unstoppable team.

> **collaborate** (*v*): to work together to produce something

Walter and I **assented** to keep it down a bit this semester.

> **assent** (*v*): agree, accept

BRAINS

YOUR TURN

Indicate whether the pairs of words below have similar or different meanings.

1. acrimonious   bitter
2. nefarious   well-meaning
3. disdain   mock
4. deleterious   helpful
5. obtuse   dull
6. intricate   complex
7. assent   concur
8. erudite   simple-minded
9. voluble   shy
10. incontrovertible   impossible to prove

In each of the groups below, choose the word that does not belong.

11. enmity   perspicacity   spite   rancor
12. disparage   malign   praise   mock
13. obdurate   stubborn   intractable   erudite
14. acquiescent   deleterious   inimical   injurious
15. pugnacious   savvy   contentious   disputatious

Choose the word that best completes the sentence.

16. My brothers made a(n) _____ mess of dinner last night. It took them longer to scrape all the burnt stuff off the pans than it did to cook the thing.

    (A) didactic (B) execrable (C) obdurate (D) polemical

17. Walter picks on me out of pure _____; he has no good reason to be so obnoxious.

    (A) erudition (B) acuteness (C) spite (D) pedagogy

18. My history teacher is a total _____. He hates it when anyone questions his theories.
    (A) doctrinaire (B) miscreant (C) charlatan (D) intelligentsia

19. My brothers and I like to _____ about everything. After all, it would be a crime to agree about anything with my lame little brothers.
    (A) remonstrate (B) disdain (C) concur (D) collaborate

20. My father hated the *Matrix* movies, and complained about them loudly and _____.
    (A) presumptuously (B) obtusely (C) acquiescently (D) virulently

21. The politician tried desperately to _____ the scandalous news about his affair.
    (A) degenerate (B) suppress (C) concur (D) assent

22. Janet is always very _____ with her words. She carefully considers everything she says.
    (A) disputatious (B) pernicious (C) deliberate (D) didactic

23. Janet and I want to _____ on a children's book someday: I'll write the text and she'll do the illustrations.
    (A) concur (B) collaborate (C) acquiesce (D) disdain

24. I told my dad his argument was completely _____ and couldn't possibly be supported.
    (A) untenable (B) incontrovertible (C) intractable (D) execrable

25. I found it awfully _____ that my grandfather expected me to settle down and have a family after high school. What century are we living in again?
    (A) obdurate (B) savvy (C) presumptuous (D) polemical

BRAINS

CHAPTER 9

HOW TO TALK ABOUT
WAITING AND LYING

My dad drove me to the big Merrill Lynch building downtown. I wanted to drive myself, but he insisted that I needed to maintain all my energy for the big interview. I wanted to tell him he was freaking me out so much it was actually *draining* my energy, but I didn't. Dad was gripping the wheel so tightly his knuckles were turning white. I couldn't very well tell him *now* that I hated the idea of this interview. And I *really* couldn't tell him that I wasn't even sure I wanted to go to college next year. Dad was an Ivy Leaguer, and the thought of his firstborn not being interested in college would be about as weird as . . . well, about as weird as her wanting to shave her head.

"Okay, sweetheart. Now, I don't want you to get too nervous," he said, trying unsuccessfully to sound soothing, "but this interview could very well determine the rest of your life."

"Thanks, Dad. Real calming."

He turned to look me in the eye. "Please, Alex, take this seriously."

"*Dad*! Watch the road!" I screamed, as a little blue-haired lady wandered out in front of our Toyota. My dad yelled something unprintable and then swung the car around.

"Sorry, I'm just nervous."

"Dad, *you're* not the one taking this interview, so stop it."

I made him sit in the car while I went inside. I was interviewing with J. D. Weston, a big-shot alum. I sat down in a chair and tried my best to look like dignified college material, even though my stomach was imitating a fleet of Olympic gymnasts going through their floor routines. I checked out my reflection in the mirror—crap. That cowlick was still there. I tried to smooth it down but my hair was being uncooperative. Finally, the receptionist led me into Weston's office.

Weston was tall and imposing, with a shock of white hair and an expensive suit. He looked at my spiky hair, frowned, and wrote something down in his notebook. *Great*, I thought. *I haven't even opened my mouth and I've got a strike against me.*

Things went downhill from there. He asked me what my hobbies were, so I told him I liked to read poetry at a club downtown. He raised his eyebrows and barked, "Anything else? Sports? Student government?" I babbled something about writing for the newspaper every once in a while, but that I didn't have a regular staff position. He asked about work experience, and I said I worked in a fast-food restaurant.

"I handle a deep fryer really well," I joked, but he wasn't laughing.

Finally, he turned to my essay. "Frankly," he said, "if my daughter came home with a shaved head, I'd probably behave just like your father."

At this point I was so tired of his attitude I just said, "Well, then, it's probably a good thing you're not my father." He frowned one last time and scribbled on his pad again before showing me out the door.

Dad was sitting on the hood of the car, looking eager. "Well? How did it go?"

"Rotten," I muttered as I got in the car. "Maybe I'll just never go to college."

Dad looked crestfallen. "Oh, Alex," he sighed, as he got into the driver's seat. "You're so smart. I just don't get it." I slumped further in my seat and didn't talk the whole way home.

*　　*　　*　　*　　*

WORDS ABOUT WAITING

I found it hard to **endure** my time in the waiting room—all I wanted to do was get out of there.

   endure (*v*): to painfully wait or suffer through something

RELATED WORDS

bide (*v*): to wait until something happens; usually used in the phrase "to *bide* one's time"

tarry (*v*): to wait idly

linger (*v*): to stick around some place because you're reluctant to go

stall (*v*): to delay someone or something

loiter (*v*): to stand around with no obvious purpose

I had **qualms** about meeting Weston. What if my outfit wasn't conservative enough? Maybe I shouldn't have worn my combat boots . . .

qualm (*n*): a nervous feeling

I tried to keep the **timorous** shake out of my voice as I introduced myself to the receptionist, but I couldn't really hide my **apprehension**.

timorous (*adj*): nervous

apprehension (*n*): fear, nervousness

I thought I saw a look of **consternation** cross her face—maybe she thought I shouldn't have worn the combat boots, either.

consternation (*n*): confusion and dismay

I'm not normally a **fretful** person, but this was an unusual circumstance.

fretful (*adj*): tending to be nervous or easily agitated

As I sat there drumming my fingers on the table, I had a **presentiment** that something huge was going to happen as soon as I walked into the office.

presentiment (*n*): a feeling that you know what's going to happen

If you have a presentiment that something specifically bad is going to happen, you're experiencing **trepidation** or **foreboding**.

trepidation (*n*): fear of something about to come

foreboding (*n*): a sense that something bad is about to happen

Man, I really wanted that receptionist to **expedite** this whole process for me, but she seemed to have no intention of doing anything but filing her nails.

expedite (*v*): to speed something up

I tried to **quell** the awful butterflies in my stomach by reciting Beatles lyrics to myself in Spanish.

quell (*v*): to soothe

Here are some synonyms for *quell*:

> **assuage** (*v*): to provide relief
> **palliate** (*v*): to provide relief
> **ameliorate** (*v*): to improve something
> **mitigate** (*v*): to make something less harsh or violent

These four words have to do with making something easier or more manageable; *quell* has the added emphasis of actually bringing the harshness to an end. For example: "He managed to *quell* the angry mob, and sent all the protestors back home."

I tightly clutched my personal **talisman**—a purple rabbit's foot my mom gave me when I was seven—which I kept in my coat pocket for good luck.

> **talisman** (*n*): an object believed to have magical powers

Whenever I gripped it, I was filled with a deep sense of **tranquility**.

> **tranquility** (*n*): peace, calm

WORDS ABOUT INTERVIEWS

Weston was very **curt** throughout the interview, which made him seem very short-tempered.

> **curt** (*adj*): rude, abrupt

Janet is a fantastic interviewee. I wish I had her sense of **aplomb**, but I always get really sweaty palms and have a tendency to crack awful, nervous jokes.

> **aplomb** (*n*): grace and style in the face of a challenge

I did manage to maintain my **equanimity** throughout, even when the guy asked me some really personal questions that I thought were pretty rude.

> **equanimity** (*n*): evenness of temper, composure

The questions were so surprising and coming so fast, I felt totally **ambushed**.

> **ambush** (*v*): to attack by surprise

When I tried to weasel my way out of an uncomfortable question, he would **probe** that subject even more.

>   **probe** (*v*): to search thoroughly

RELATED WORDS

He **scrutinized** me coldly, as if I were an inanimate object being **appraised** and not a human being.

>   **scrutinize** (*v*): to examine extremely carefully
>   **appraise** (*v*): to judge the value or worth of something

I mean, what kind of **inquisition** was this?

>   **inquisition** (*n*): a harsh or unfair investigation

He gave me a **disparaging** look when I told him I liked to perform in poetry slams. Apparently, he didn't find that too impressive.

>   **disparaging** (*adj*): showing disapproval

I had practiced offering clear, succinct answers that were quick but didn't seem too **perfunctory**.

>   **perfunctory** (*adj*): quick, brief, shallow

The interviewer's questions were totally **arbitrary** and random. First he was asking me about my poetry, then all of a sudden he was asking me for my thoughts on the Middle East.

>   **arbitrary** (*adj*): chosen without any particular logic

At one point he asked me, "If you had to choose, would you rather have gills or antennae?" I told him I wasn't exactly sure how to solve that particular **conundrum**, but I guessed gills would be easier to hide under clothing.

>   **conundrum** (*n*): puzzle or riddle

I meant that as a **quip**, but he just seemed confused.

>   **quip** (*n*): short, witty remark

All my attempts to make the guy laugh fell flat; I tried to seem **serene**, but it really bothered me.

>   **serene** (*adj*): calm, unworried

My performance was far from **impeccable**, but I thought I did okay, considering.

>   **impeccable** (*adj*): perfect

WORDS ABOUT LYING

I wasn't *exactly* lying when I said I never got a B in my life; I was just being **equivocal.** I mean, I got a C once, but that wasn't a B!

> **equivocal** (*adj*): manipulating the truth just enough to avoid lying outright

RELATED WORDS

Here are other words that can be used to describe sneaking around the truth.

Weston's expression was **ambiguous**—I couldn't tell if he thought I was funny, charming, strange, or all of the above.

> **ambiguous** (*adj*): unclear; having more than one interpretation

The interviewer looked at my spiky haircut and, after a moment, said it was "interesting." Which, of course, is a **euphemism** for "downright strange."

> **euphemism** (*n*): a polite way of saying something distasteful

When he asked me why I wanted to go to this school, I went on a big **circumlocution** about college in general, just to avoid talking about it. After all, I'm still not sure I even want to go there!

> **circumlocution** (*n*): using more words than necessary in order to avoid saying something directly

I didn't want to use some **hyperbole** like "If I don't go to your school, I'll die."

> **hyperbole** (*n*): extreme exaggeration

I told Weston that my legal name was Alex, not Alexandra, because my parents thought I was going to be a boy. The story's probably **apocryphal**, but my dad likes to tell it anyway.

> **apocryphal** (*adj*): probably not true, but generally believed to be true

I would never write anything **fallacious** in my application.

> **fallacious** (*adj*): false, deceptive

I want a school to accept the real me, not some **spurious** version of myself.

> **spurious** (*adj*): being different from what it claims to be

I think I answered everything honestly. I didn't bother being **devious** in any of my answers—except about that C.

   devious (*adj*): insincere, dishonest

I'd swear as to the **veracity** of everything in there.

   veracity (*n*): the truth

The antonym of *veracity* is **mendacity** (*n*): a lie.

If I get into that school after all, though, I'll swear it was a case of **chicanery**.

   chicanery (*n*): trickery

At the end of our interview, Weston made no sign that would **divulge** what he thought of me.

   divulge (*v*): to reveal

YOUR TURN

Match the vocab words on the left with their definitions on the right.

1.	talisman	a.	to attack with surprise
2.	quip	b.	a major exaggeration
3.	conundrum	c.	dishonesty
4.	hyperbole	d.	rude, rushed
5.	mendacity	e.	to hurry something along
6.	foreboding	f.	to judge the value of
7.	ambush	g.	a short, witty comment
8.	curt	h.	a presentiment of something bad
9.	expedite	i.	a lucky charm
10.	appraise	j.	a puzzle

In each of the groups below, choose the word that does not belong.

11. timorous   apprehensive   fretful   relaxed
12. ameliorate   mitigate   anger   assuage
13. fallacious   perfunctory   spurious   false
14. tranquility   equanimity   consternation   composure
15. palliate   scrutinize   probe   investigate

From the list below, select the word that best describes each person portrayed in the phrases that follow.

devious   perfunctory   unequivocal   disparaging   serene   loitering
assuaging   arbitrary   impeccable   timorous

16. Someone who stays cool while her boss is yelling at her
17. Someone who hides in the back of the classroom and hates being called on
18. Someone who never has a hair out of place
19. Someone who sits in the corner at a party, saying nasty things about everyone else's outfit/date/hygiene
20. Someone who always expresses his opinions straightforwardly

WAITING AND LYING

21. Someone who knows how to get away with cutting class
22. Someone hanging out in front of the 7-Eleven©, with nowhere better to go
23. Someone who is calming a screaming child in the supermarket
24. Someone who spends the ten minutes before class doing her homework
25. Someone who decides to wear a tuxedo to school for no apparent reason

‑ HAPTER 1‑‑
HOW TO TALK ABOUT
SELF‑EXPRESSION

A few weeks later, things still weren't much better with my dad. He was upset because he thought I deliberately threw the interview. I told him that wasn't true, but yeah, maybe I wasn't so hot about the idea of college, and maybe the interviewer picked up on that. That threw him into another fit, and he started going on and on about what happens to kids who don't go to college, how I'd never have a future, yadda yadda yadda. Mike and Wayne got a big kick out of it all, because normally they're the ones getting yelled at by Dad. I just tried to hang out at Janet's house as much as possible.

Tonight, though, I was feeling better. The last Friday of the month is always open mic night at the Tin Cup, and I was ready with two new poems. The first one was something I wrote for Ms. Lieberman's class. It was all about youth and confusion and indecision, and I called it "My Hamlet Days." (Okay, so, maybe it's a little conceited to compare yourself to the greatest character in English literature . . . but I'm a poet. So sue me.) The second was all about being in love with someone gorgeous and unattainable. I didn't put in enough details to identify Rex, but I couldn't resist adding a line about the way his hands looked holding a guitar.

All the regulars were reading that night, and there was a great community vibe. I loved how different all the writers were at the Cup. There were people who rapped, people who wrote long political rants, and that night there was even one guy who improvised his poetry over a jazz quartet. During a DJ break I was talking to Maryam, one of the rappers, when I saw a familiar face. Rex was wearing a black zip-up hoodie and had his hands jammed in his pockets. He looked like he was waiting for something. I looked over my shoulder, expecting to see one of his bandmates. When I turned around again, he gave me a crooked little smile.

Maryam had discreetly disappeared at that point. I sputtered for a bit, looking for support, but before I knew it Rex was walking over to me and there was nothing I could do. "Hey," he said.

"Hey," I managed to say back. Okay, not a bad start. I looked down: no boobs in sight.

"Tom the DJ mentioned you read here sometimes." Tom saw me and flashed the thumbs-up sign from his turntables. I blushed like a tomato and tried to cover it up by coughing really loudly.

"Yeah, isn't that funny? I mean, you play music here, I read poetry here. . . ." The sentence trailed off, letting my total lack of coolness hang in the air for all to witness. He laughed anyway.

"You should call me sometime," he said suddenly. He pulled out a card with the Giants' logo on the back and scribbled a number. "Maybe we could, I don't know, play music and read poetry," he smiled. "Call me next week, okay?" And just like it was nothing, he walked off, leaving me holding the card and trying to not to squeal like a twelve-year-old.

* * * * *

WORDS ABOUT READING POETRY

The first poet read a really **florid** poem about her boyfriend that made me want to retch. Bet you he was pretty embarrassed too.

florid (*adj*): flowery, overdone

I hate poets who give really **histrionic** performances, and flail all over the place while shouting and throwing things.

histrionic (*adj*): overdramatic

RELATED WORDS

The following words can be used to describe people's speaking voices.

Charles is a really **emphatic** reader; he takes his time and gives very commanding performances.

emphatic (*adj*): forcible, definite

He has very crisp **enunciation**—you can always understand exactly what he's saying.

> **enunciation** (*n*): the clarity of one's pronunciation

His **stentorian** voice makes him sound way older than he really is.

> **stentorian** (*adj*): loud and powerful in tone

Mara, on the other hands, is a totally **phlegmatic** performer. She always sounds like she's reading her grocery list.

> **phlegmatic** (*adj*): without emotion

That's better than Nitin, though, who tends to read his poems with this completely **affected** British accent. For God's sake, the boy was born in St. Louis!

> **affected** (*adj*): behaving unnaturally with the intention of impressing other people

Sometimes his poetry gets really **sententious** and preachy, but you can forgive him because it's really good.

> **sententious** (*adj*): overly moralizing

I like the open mic night at the Tin Cup because you can hear so many different **genres** of poetry in one evening—from dirty political limericks to classical sonnets to completely free-form poems.

> **genre** (*n*): category of literature or art (for example: crime novels, romances, and fantasies are all various *genres* of fiction.)

Young-soon's poems are incredibly complex and **nuanced**—you can hear them over and over again and learn something new each time.

> **nuanced** (*adj*): filled with slight, understated shades of meaning

I want to get a copy of her poems, so I can read them and see what **subtle** things I missed.

> **subtle** (*adj*): not obvious; understated

Watching her perform her poems is really **revelatory**, because you'd never think such amazing stuff would come from such a quiet girl.

> **revelatory** (*adj*): expressing something not known before

Lots of people try to **emulate** her style, but they can never match her.

> **emulate** (*v*): to mimic

I find reading my poetry to be **therapeutic**. It helps me express myself in a safe way.

    therapeutic (*adj*): an activity that is healing

Marlon, the MC, is a total **raconteur**. He's a stand-up comedian the other days of the week, and it totally shows.

    raconteur (*n*): an entertaining storyteller

At the end of the year I want to put together an **anthology** of Tin Cup writers, to raise money for the event.

    anthology (*n*): collection of literary works by various authors

WORDS ABOUT CRUSHES AND ACCIDENTAL ENCOUNTERS

Most of my crushes have been short-lived, **evanescent** things.

    evanescent (*adj*): fleeting

Those crushes are usually **illusory** and based on nothing, but this one is for real. I think.

    illusory (*adj*): like an illusion; not real

I did my best to seem totally **nonchalant** when Rex came up to talk to me, but I don't think I did a very good job of it.

    nonchalant (*adj*): breezy, unconcerned

RELATED WORDS

When he complimented my poetry, I tried to be **flippant** about it—as if it were just a hobby, and not my passion in life.

    flippant (*adj*): inappropriately casual

SELF-EXPRESSION

I didn't even have to **insinuate** that we should go on a date—he totally beat me to it.

insinuate (*v*): to get into a position gradually; to suggest

I kind of liked not having to **languish** and wait around, wondering if he was going to ask me out.

languish (*v*): to suffer as a result of being denied something

Rex didn't even pretend it was just a **fortuitous** meeting. He actually admitted he came to see me!

fortuitous (*adj*): happening by chance, lucky

I knew something good was going to happen today—the twelfth of the month is always an **auspicious** time for me.

auspicious (*adj*): marked by lucky signs

All in all, it seemed like a **propitious** meeting, even though I still feel like a moron in front of him.

propitious (*adj*): favorable

I'll admit, I had been **furtively** looking around all night to see if he would show up.

furtively (*adv*): done in a way that attempts to escape notice

When he finally did come talk to me, I almost spilled my Snapple all over his shoes. Miss **Maladroit**, as always.

maladroit (*adj*): clumsy, inept

I also seemed to have lost all ability to talk like a normal person. He complimented me, and all I could do was mumble **inarticulate** nonsense.

inarticulate (*adj*): unable to speak clearly or choose the right words

He very **tactfully** ignored my stupid remarks.

tactfully (*adv*): not rudely; done with concern for other people's feelings

I admit it—I have a **penchant** for mumbly indie rockers.

penchant (*n*): a strong tendency toward or liking for

For a moment onstage, I got lost in a **reverie**, thinking about me, Rex, and the cute pierced children we would have.

reverie (*n*): getting lost in happy thoughts about something

SELF-EXPRESSION

I was in a state of **oblivion** for a second before realizing I was still onstage.
oblivion (*n*): a complete state of nothingness or forgetting

Normally I'm pretty **circumspect** about boys. Who can trust a seventeen-year-old boy, after all?
circumspect (*adj*): unwilling to act without weighing all the consequences

Janet keeps warning me to be **wary**, but not too wary.
wary (*adj*): cautious

I'm trying not to do anything **impetuous**.
impetuous (*adj*): hasty, done without thought

But then, **spontaneity** is what being a teenager is supposed to be all about, right?
spontaneity (*n*): actions done on the spur of the moment

I keep getting lost in **whimsical** thoughts about Rex and me going out.
whimsical (*adj*): fanciful, imaginative

But then I have to be **pragmatic**. I don't want to count my chickens before they're hatched!
pragmatic (*adj*): practical, concerned with results

I think about Rex **relentlessly**.
relentlessly (*adv*): continuously, without lessening or slacking

He practically **exudes** sex appeal.
exude (*v*): to emit, to ooze out slowly

I can imagine the two of us living in **connubial** bliss. Ew, not now! But someday . . .
connubial (*adj*): relating to marriage

When I see him, my heart goes into little **paroxysms** of joy.
paroxysm (*n*): sudden outburst of emotion

I love him **ardently** and wholeheartedly.
ardently (*adv*): done with heartfelt sincerity

When he smiles at me with those crooked teeth, I'm totally **elated** and thrown into a state of **jubilation**.
elated (*adj*): overjoyed
jubilation (*n*): incredible joy

We're definitely **compatible**. We have the same hi-top Converse sneakers. If that's not love, I don't know what is.

compatible (*adj*): go well together

I have all kinds of **amorous** thoughts about Rex that make me blush a little.

amorous (*adj*): lustful

I've always wanted to have a **carnal** relationship with a musician. Blame MTV for all those **wanton** music videos!

carnal (*adj*): sensual, sexual

wanton (*adj*): unrestrained and unruly (usually related to sexual behavior)

All sorts of **lurid** things went through my head the next day. Maybe this was all some kind of awful trick!

lurid (*adj*): sensationalistic

YOUR TURN

Indicate whether the pairs of words below have similar or different meanings.

1. wary   circumspect
2. evanescent   long-lasting
3. ardent   affected
4. emulate   imitate
5. subtle   nuanced
6. inarticulate   talkative
7. carnal   amorous
8. exude   insinuate
9. phlegmatic   emphatic
10. relentlessly   unendingly

From the list below, select the word that best describes the couple portrayed in the phrases that follow.

furtive   connubial   histrionic   compatible   impetuous

11. Two people who have the same taste in music, movies, books, and politics
12. A newlywed couple
13. A couple whose parents don't approve of their dating, forcing them to sneak around and meet in secret
14. A couple who drives down to Mexico one Saturday for no good reason
15. The couple that's always having huge fights at the local Starbucks

Choose the word that best completes the sentence.

16. No matter how cool my brothers pretend to be, they get totally tongue-tied and _____ in front of girls.
    (A) tactful (B) inarticulate (C) flippant (D) nuanced

17. The tabloid magazine was filled with _____ gossip about minor celebrities.
     (A) therapeutic (B) stentorian (C) lurid (D) maladroit

18. I love reading children's books, because they're so _____ and imaginative. They take me back to a more innocent time.
     (A) whimsical (B) connubial (C) spontaneous (D) aloof

19. Martin Luther King, Jr. was a powerful speaker with a _____ voice.
     (A) florid (B) therapeutic (C) propitious (D) stentorian

20. I enjoy reading many different _____ of literature, not just poetry.
     (A) nuances (B) genres (C) paroxysms (D) anthologies

21. It was a(n) _____ coincidence that I found a twenty-dollar bill on the sidewalk *just* when I was thinking about buying the new Alicia Keys album.
     (A) illusory (B) elated (C) wanton (D) fortuitous

22. The other day, I was walking around in a total state of _____ and walked right into a telephone pole.
     (A) oblivion (B) jubilation (C) wariness (D) spontaneity

23. When I was complaining about being broke last fall, my father subtly _____ that I should go out and get a job.
     (A) exuded (B) languished (C) emulated (D) insinuated

24. Bill Cosby is a great _____. He could read the phone book and make it amusing.
     (A) oblivion (B) reverie (C) raconteur (D) anthology

25. Some parents don't let their kids watch R-rated movies because they're concerned about all the inappropriately _____ bits.
     (A) carnal (B) ardent (C) maladroit (D) auspicious

CHAPTER 11
HOW TO TALK ABOUT
COLLEGE AND PARTYING

That weekend, I drove down to San Diego with Janet, who wanted to check out a college there. She'd pretty much already been accepted—big surprise—and they were hinting that she was going to get some heavy science scholarship. I was tired of my dad being on my case all the time, so I tagged along. He was happy I was at least showing some vague interest in a school, so it created some peace in the house.

We had a good time driving down in Janet's mom's old minivan, with the windows down and Janis Joplin playing really loudly on the stereo. We drank Capri-Suns, and Janet tried to rewrite all the lyrics to "Bobby McGee" to be about Rex and me. By the time we got there, I was in a much better mood.

The campus was gorgeous, in that way that only California colleges can be. Tall trees, beautiful Spanish-style buildings, and kids playing Frisbee even though it was almost winter. Janet took one look at it and was obviously head over heels. I was happy to see her so excited, but when I looked around, it didn't do much for me. I wasn't sure why, but I didn't want to spend the next four years of my life stuck at school. Again. And frat parties? I'll pass, thanks. Janet had heard about one going on that night, though, and she begged me to come with her, so I suppose I can say I've been to *one* in my life.

Janet had a meeting with the head of the chem department, so I told her I'd wander around and meet up with her later. I walked past the big, fancy buildings and around the wide green courtyards until I came to the English department. Well, I thought. Might as well look around.

The place was pretty quiet when I walked in, but one office had its door wide open. I thought I heard . . . wait, no, it couldn't be. Was that the Roots I heard blasting out the doorway? Curious, I walked down the hallway. A woman in her thirties was sitting in the office, banging on her desk in time with the music. She saw me and smiled. "Sorry, was I being too loud? I can turn it down."

"No, no," I said. "I was just visiting the campus, and was wondering what kind of English professor listens to loud hip-hop."

She laughed. "This one does." She introduced herself as Professor Wexler and invited me in. I ended up spending an hour with her in the office. We started talking about music and poetry, and the conversation just flowed from there. She was *awesome*. Eventually I felt comfortable enough admitting that I wasn't really feeling the college vibe at the moment.

She put her arms behind her head. "So don't go right away," she said. "I didn't."

"Really? Then what did you do?" I asked.

She laughed loudly and said, "Drove around in a van with my boyfriend for a few months. He was a band photographer. But eventually I realized he was nothing but bad news, so I ditched him and went to Kenya for a year." A light bulb went off in my head at that point. A year abroad . . . I wanted to stay and talk to Professor Wexler some more, but I had to go meet Janet to (ugh) get ready for this party. But she gave me her email address, and as I left her office, my brain was already leafing through imaginary travel brochures.

*   *   *   *   *

WORDS ABOUT COLLEGE

The library looked like an old Gothic church on the outside. It really felt like a **hallowed** place.

    hallowed (*adj*): holy, blessed

The book stacks, however, had all been **desecrated** by graffiti.

    desecrate (*v*): to ruin something sacred

All the buildings on campus were referred to by their **abbreviated** names; John M. Carver Hall became JMC.

    abbreviate (*v*): to shorten

The old oaks in the courtyard represented the college's **longevity**.

    longevity (*n*): length of life

The English department was the home of many **venerable** professors.

> **venerable** (*adj*): respectable, usually because of age

Venerability made a lot of them rather **pompous**; none of them had time to talk to a lowly prospective student.

> **pompous** (*adj*): conceited, self-important

The **stodgy** old professors turned me off, but I suppose they'd worked hard to earn being antisocial.

> **stodgy** (*adj*): old-fashioned, stuffy, plodding

The tour guide kept telling us that only a **rarefied** group of students gets the chance to attend this university.

rarified or **rarefied** (*adj*): only the best, separated from what is coarse or ordinary

They used test scores, grades, and letters of recommendation to **cull** the group they wanted.

> **cull** (*v*): to separate the desirable from the undesirable

The tour guide tried to be as **restrained** as possible, as if to suggest this was a dignified, serious place for mature students.

> **restrained** (*adj*): controlled, not showing too much emotion

Last year, because of a large grant, the college was able to replace their **obsolete** computers with brand-new ones.

> **obsolete** (*adj*): old-fashioned, replaced by something newer

The grant had been made by a group of recent **alumni** who had formed a successful software company.

> **alumni** (*n*): graduates of a particular school. The feminine single form is *alumna*; the masculine single form is *alumnus*.

Many rich alumni choose to **bequeath** things to the school.

> **bequeath** (*v*): to leave something to a person or institution after death

One **philanthropist** donated enough money for the school to build a state-of-the-art, high-powered telescope.

> **philanthropist** (*n*): someone dedicated to charitable works

College doesn't have the same **hierarchy** that high school has. Here, it's okay for freshmen and seniors to hang out together.

> **hierarchy** (*n*): a system that ranks people

The president of the college **abdicated** after a particularly messy scandal.
abdicate (*v*): to formally give something up (usually a high office or position)

My host student was really **accommodating**—she let me sleep in her bed while she took the futon.
accommodating (*adj*): willing to adjust one's actions in order to help someone else

The dorms had plenty of **amenities**, like a full gym and dining hall in each building.
amenities (*n*): features that make a place attractive to guests or customers

The college was **aggrandizing** the size of its freshman class this year.
aggrandize (*v*): to increase the size of something

When I looked at the tuition fees for a single term, I was sure someone was getting **bilked** out of something.
bilk (*v*): to cheat

I thought you'd have to have a fancy **pedigree** to go here, but my host student is the daughter of dairy farmers from North Dakota.
pedigree (*n*): lineage

The daily happenings on campus are **chronicled** in the student newspaper.
chronicle (*v*): to record (It can also be a noun, meaning "a record.")

WORDS ABOUT A COOL PROFESSOR

Professor Wexler was considered quite a **precocious** talent; she breezed through her PhD and was made professor at a really young age.
precocious (*adj*): being smarter or more developed than is expected at a certain age

Landing a professor position at such a young age was considered quite a **coup**.
coup (*n*): an unexpected and skillful success

The younger students treated her with total **reverence**.
   reverence (*n*): extreme respect

Professor Wexler wrote an **acclaimed** book on hip-hop culture that managed to become a popular best-seller, as well.
   acclaimed (*adj*): having been praised greatly in public

People took her book as a **bellwether** that popular music was going to be an important field of study in coming years.
   bellwether (*n*): someone or something that indicates future trends

She's also an **accomplished** violinist.
   accomplished (*adj*): very skilled, talented

And she's an **avid** soccer player.
   avid (*adj*): eager, enthusiastic

Professor Wexler had the **acumen** to help navigate the tricky world of university politics.
   acumen (*n*): quick, accurate insight

Professor Wexler always has a lot of **obsequious** students hanging around her, offering to do her photocopying or get her coffee.
   obsequious (*adj*): excessively eager to please

She's so popular with her students and colleagues that her few enemies find her **unassailable**.
   unassailable (*adj*): so well-established that it cannot be challenged or
      beaten

And despite all this, I found her very **accessible**.
   accessible (*adj*): easy to approach, easy to enter

RELATED WORDS

She was **affable** and laughed easily. We spent a very **amicable** hour together.
   affable (*adj*): friendly, easy to talk to
   amicable (*adj*): friendly

I felt an **affinity** for Professor Wexler. We even liked the same bands!
   affinity (*n*): a natural liking for someone or something

She showed me it was possible to be **cerebral** and fun at the same time.
cerebral (*adj*): intellectual

WORDS ABOUT PARTYING

College is so full of **hedonists**, I'm amazed any work gets done.
hedonist (*n*): one who is devoted to pleasure and happiness

They seem to have an **insatiable** appetite for partying.
insatiable (*adj*): impossible to satisfy

Alcohol was handed out at the party I went to, in **flagrant** disobedience of the state liquor laws.
flagrant (*adj*): very obvious

I saw a girl fall asleep with her head in a toilet, and I prayed I would never reach such a state of **debasement**.
debasement (*n*): reduction in value, quality, or significance

It wasn't total **anarchy**, though; they knew well enough to keep the partying inside and off the streets.
anarchy (*n*): complete lack of rules

At some colleges, a particular amount of money is **allocated** to students for throwing parties.
allocate (*v*): to divide and hand out

College students are **incorrigible**—you'll never get them to stop, no matter how many rules you pass.
incorrigible (*adj*): unable to be reformed

Some people think the college way of life is **reprehensible**, but I think most people realize it's just part of being young and stupid.
reprehensible (*adj*): highly unacceptable

I **abstained** from smoking or drinking while I was there.
abstain (*v*): to choose not to do something

The **profligate** party throwers had blown a ton of money on ice sculptures, piñatas, and belly dancers.

    profligate (*adj*): extravagant, wasteful

Janet and I passed a drunk guy on the street who yelled some really **profane** things at us, but we ignored him and kept walking.

    profane (*adj*): vulgar, disrespectful (usually toward something holy or sacred)

The next morning, I saw more than one person who must have been **inebriated** the day before.

    inebriated (*adj*): drunk

After a week of studying hard, haven't students earned the right to **carouse** a bit?

    carouse (*v*): to drink and be merry

I liked watching happy people **cavort** in the street.

    cavort (*v*): to behave in a playful, physically lively way

Back home, my friends all wanted stories of the **turpitude** I had seen at the big college party.

    turpitude (*n*): wickedness, immorality

YOUR TURN

Match the vocab words on the left with their definitions on the right.

1.	cavort	a.	affable
2.	inebriated	b.	intellectual
3.	acclaimed	c.	sinfulness
4.	cerebral	d.	one who lives for pleasure
5.	amicable	e.	one who gives money to charity
6.	hedonist	f.	to jump around playfully
7.	chronicle	g.	highly praised
8.	profligate	h.	historical record
9.	philanthropist	i.	drunken
10.	turpitude	j.	wasteful

Choose the best word from the list given below to fill in the blanks. Not every word will be used.

hallowed   insatiable   obsequious   incorrigible   profane   venerable
longevity   amenities   hierarchy   abdicate   allocate   anarchy   coup
cull   bilk   bequeath   desecrate   precocious   unassailable   avid
accommodating

11. As soon as I walked in, I could sense that the huge cathedral was an incredibly _____ place.

12. The castle was so well guarded, the enemy army found it to be _____.

13. My brothers are _____. No matter how many times they get punished, they never learn.

14. The seven-year-old was very _____; he could already speak four languages and name all the state capitals.

15. Our school vice-principal is always following the principal around, paying him ridiculously _____ compliments.

16. The king has decided to _____ his throne in order to pursue his lifelong dream of becoming a pop music star.

17. After many years of acclaimed work, the professor was a(n) _____ man with an unassailable reputation.

18. A wheat thresher will _____ the edible wheat from the inedible stalks, leaves, and husks.

19. Someone wrote something really _____ on the walls of the girls' room. I'm not a prude, but even I blushed at it!

20. The salesman tried to _____ me out of an extra twenty dollars on the car stereo.

21. My grandmother exercises, watches her diet, and takes lots of vitamins in order to ensure her _____.

22. My brothers' appetites are _____. I'm amazed they've managed to stay so skinny.

23. When I die, I'm going to _____ my body to a laboratory.

24. I'm a(n) _____ fan of horror movies—I watch every new one that comes out.

25. I was impressed by the hotel's _____. I snagged all the little shampoo bottles I could, and I almost thought about taking the robe and slippers too.

CHAPTER 12
MORE HOMONYMS

Okay, here goes—another chapter from my brothers! This is the last one they owe me, and then I have to go back to washing the dishes again. . . .

*   *   *   *   *

Okay, we've got another story for you. This one happened just last week. Now, Mike had been jocking this girl, Fran, forever. She works at the local record store, and every day after school Mike would walk in and ask her about such-and-such cool record, in the hopes that it would spark a conversation. (*Not that he actually has good taste in music—he just keeps stealing my music magazines to pick up girls!—Alex*) Anyhow, one day it finally pays off, and Fran agrees to go out with Mike. He leaves his number and she promises to call later in the week to make plans.

When Fran finally calls, Mike isn't at home. Wayne picks up the phone, and Fran asks, "Mike?" See, Fran has no idea Mike is an identical twin. Luckily, Mike had told Wayne all about her. Wayne decides to play along for a while, so he chats her up for a few minutes. Wayne pretends he's Mike the whole time, and arranges to go see the latest Coen brothers' movie with her on Friday. When he hangs up, he realizes that this is a prime opportunity to pull a supreme prank. When Mike gets home, Wayne begs and pleads for him to play along. At first Mike doesn't want to, since he'd just worked his butt off trying to get Fran to go out with him in the first place. But finally, the wiseass in him wins out, and he agrees.

Friday night rolls around, and Mike goes to pick Fran up. Wayne, meanwhile, is already waiting at the theater, wearing the exact outfit Mike is (we keep a few sets of those around, just in case). Mike drops Fran off at the door, saying that he'll park the car and come back. Thirty seconds later, Wayne walks up to Fran and asks if she wants to go in. She does a double take, and then makes some crack about how fast that was. Wayne just shrugs and they go in and take their seats. Halfway through the previews, Wayne says he's going to get some popcorn. Mike, of course, is waiting outside the door with a huge bucket of popcorn and some Junior Mints, for good measure. Fran is definitely a little weirded out at this point, and it doesn't get any better when Mike gets up to go to the bathroom, only to return fifteen seconds later with his fly unzipped and toilet paper stuck to his shoe (a particularly brilliant touch, we thought.) Finally, the movie ends and Wayne goes off to get the car. Actually, though, he runs behind the theater just as Mike drives up in the car. For a second, we think Fran wasn't going to get in the car—she looks so, totally, completely freaked at this point. But she does, and she calms down a bit as Mike sweet-talks her.

That is, she calms down until Wayne comes flying out of the bushes and throws himself on the windshield of the car.

Fran screams bloody murder, and we burst into laughter like a bunch of idiots—we were practically holding our sides in. Fran, though, didn't find it so funny. She totally let one fly at Mike, and he had a black eye for a week after. (Note to selves: Never pull pranks on girls with black belts.)

Mike's waiting for the eye to heal before asking her on a second date.

*   *   *   *   *

Okay, you know the drill—here are some more homonyms for you.

*   *   *   *   *

MORE HOMONYMS

I told my brothers that they couldn't use my special, expensive **stationery** to write out their grocery list, and that if I found it had moved from its **stationary** position on my desk there would be hell to pay.

    stationery (*n*): writing materials

    stationary (*adj*): fixed, unmoving

My father believes in the **principle** of working for what you get. In fact, I would say that's probably his **principal** belief—he puts it above all others.

    principle (*n*): rule, standard

    principal (*adj*): chief, foremost (also, of course, as a noun it means the guy at your school who makes all the rules)

I needed to find my copy of *Hamlet* before I could write my essay, because I wanted to **cite** the professor who had written the introduction. However, it seemed my brothers had moved my book to some other **site**.

cite (*v*): to quote someone as an authority

site (*n*): place, location

My brothers often **flout** my father's rules, and then **flaunt** it at school—they like having reputations for being bad-asses.

flout (*v*): to openly disobey

flaunt (*v*): to show off

When my brothers told me that **incredible** story about meeting Britney Spears at our local mall, I have to admit I was pretty **incredulous**.

incredible (*adj*): something so surprising or unusual it almost can't be believed

incredulous (*adj*): unable to believe something

My brothers often use their sweet, **ingenuous** appearance to fool people—you'd never think such nice-looking boys would actually be such devious, **ingenious** troublemakers.

ingenuous (*adj*): innocent, inexperienced

ingenious (*adj*): extremely clever

My brothers **loathe** doing chores. They are especially **loath** to clean the bathroom, even though they're the only ones who mess it up.

loathe (*v*): to hate, despise

loath (*adj*): to be unwilling to do something

I mean, it's certainly not my fault there's always an **odorous** haze around the bathroom. It's an **odious** task, but they have to take responsibility.

odorous (*adj*): awful smelling

odious (*adj*): hateful

My brothers could clean the bathroom **alternately**; one week Mike could do it, then Wayne the next. **Alternatively**, they could do it together each week.

alternately (*adv*): one after the other, in turn

alternatively (*adv*): on the other hand

When he left for a business trip last month, my **perspicacious** father knew that he needed to leave very clear, **perspicuous** instructions for my brothers if he wanted the dog and plants to be alive when he got back.

perspicacious (*adj*): wise, insightful
perspicuous (*adj*): easily understood

Our principal, Mr. Limbergh, has a **plenitude** of **platitudes** that he likes whipping out for all occasions. His favorite is "Haste makes waste," which he yells at people who run in the halls.

plenitude (*n*): abundance, plenty
platitude (*n*): a trite, overused saying

At Mississippi Fried Chicken, some employees get year-end bonuses. However, the **prerequisite** for getting that **perquisite** is working at MFC for two full years—a task I'm not sure I'm up for.

prerequisite (*n*): a condition that must be met before beginning something
perquisite (*n*): a perk or privilege given in addition to one's salary

Mike kept putting off his English essay, so as a **stimulus** my dad said he would buy Mike a case of Coke, his favorite **stimulant**, if he managed to write the first page that night.

stimulus (*n*): something that encourages something to begin or develop
stimulant (*n*): a substance that causes excitement (caffeine, some narcotics, etc.)

My brothers wished they lived in an **amoral** universe, where their **immoral** behavior wouldn't be a problem.

amoral (*adj*): unconcerned with morals
immoral (*adj*): acts against accepted morals

The difference here is that the first word describes something lacking any kind of moral system, good or bad. The second describes a specifically *negative* moral system.

Whenever I'm fighting with my brothers, Dad tries to be a **disinterested** judge and come up with the fairest solution. He always takes time to listen to us, even if he's totally **uninterested** in what we're talking about.

disinterested (*adj*): without bias; impartial
uninterested (*adj*): lacking interest in something

My brothers usually do a pretty **unexceptional** job on their homework—they always land right in the middle of a class. My dad wants them to get straight A's, but my brothers think their performance is **unexceptionable**.

unexceptional (*adj*): not special
unexceptionable (*adj*): good enough, with no apparent reason for complaint

Right now, my brothers' stupid acts are pretty **venial.** However, Dad worries about them going to college, which is a hotbed of much more **venal** behavior.

venial (*adj*): minor, easily excused
venal (*adj*): corruptible

Don't confuse either of these words with **venereal** (*adj*): spread through sexual contact. Hmm, major social embarrassment is possible with that mix-up!

If my brothers had the power to become **invisible**, they'd be **invincible**—they'd never get caught.

invisible (*adj*): unable to be seen
invincible (*adj*): impossible to defeat or destroy

When I was eleven I blamed my brothers for **dissolving** my science fair project, a jar of dirt that I'd been keeping the fridge. They were **absolved** when my dad confessed he'd mistakenly washed the jar out.

dissolve (*v*): to break down in water; to fade away and disappear
absolve (*v*): to clear someone of guilt

When my brothers think a waitress is cute, they usually leave her a **gratuitously** large **gratuity**.

gratuitous (*adj*): unnecessary
gratuity (*n*): extra money given for a service; a tip

At the last school dance, I watched my brother **oscillate** between these two freshman girls before finally deciding to **osculate** one of them. It was totally disgusting.

oscillate (*v*): to swing between two points
osculate (*v*): to kiss

Walter is so sure of himself, he's convinced that his admission to that **eminent** Ivy League college is **imminent**.

eminent (*adj*): important, distinguished, respected
imminent (*adj*): about to happen any minute

MORE HOMONYMS

My brothers are totally **edacious**, and when they're eating they lose any concern for manners that they ever had. I'm always shocked by their **audacious** behavior in restaurants. They don't care who's watching as they shovel it in.

    edacious (*adj*): voracious, loving to eat

    audacious (*adj*): bold, unconcerned with authority

When they were little, my brothers were **inveterate** torturers of small **invertebrates**.

    inveterate (*adj*): unable to be changed (generally applied to a bad habit)

    invertebrate (*n*): an animal without a spine (like a worm)

My father thought that getting my brothers a tutor might **affect** their grades, but so far it doesn't seem to have had any **effect**.

    affect (*v*): to change, to influence

    effect (*n*): result, outcome

YOUR TURN

Match the vocab words on the left with their definitions on the right.

1.	flout	a.	a tip
2.	flaunt	b.	can't be reformed
3.	venal	c.	to go back and forth
4.	venial	d.	to shamelessly disobey
5.	oscillate	e.	minor
6.	osculate	f.	can't be seen
7.	inveterate	g.	impartial
8.	invertebrate	h.	to kiss
9.	loath	i.	animal without a backbone
10.	loathe	j.	can't be beaten
11.	uninterested	k.	to show off
12.	disinterested	l.	unwilling
13.	invincible	m.	unnecessary
14.	invisible	n.	corruptible
15.	gratuitous	o.	to hate
16.	gratuity	p.	lacking interest

Choose the best word from the list given below to fill in the blanks. Not every word will be used.

odious   odorous   unexceptionable   unexceptional   plenitude   platitude
incredulous   incredible   stimulus   stimulant   absolve   dissolve   imminent
eminent   cite   site

17. In biology class, we had the _____ task of cutting up a nasty, dead frog.

18. Coffee is a _____.

19. My uncle loves red meat and greasy, fried foods. The way he eats, I fear that a heart attack is _____.

20. After I turned in my essay, I realized that I had accidentally numbered the pages wrong. Oh well. That's not a big deal—the paper is still

    _____.

21. I did remember to _____ some major authorities in my essay.

22. When my dad found out it was my brothers—not me—who broke the lamp, he had to _____ me.

23. I like little kids because they're never _____. You can tell them anything and they'll believe you.

24. Wayne forgot to take out the garbage last week, and soon a(n) _____ smell was collecting in the kitchen.

25. It's a shame that, given the _____ of food we're used to in the United States, some people in the world go to bed hungry.

CHAPTER 13
HOW TO TALK ABOUT TRAVEL AND ADVENTURE

"So, traveling, huh? Wicked."

Rex and I were waiting outside Los Feliz, a theater downtown. I had had the little card taped on my mirror for a week before Janet finally convinced me to just phone him up already. When I called, he said his favorite band, Modest Mouse, was playing that weekend and that I should come with him to the concert. "I promise, you'll love them," he said.

"How would you know what I'd love? You barely know me," I teased.

He thought for a moment and then answered, "Well, they're cool. And you seem cool. Therefore, I pronounce a perfect fit!" I told him flattery would get him everywhere and that I'd meet him at Los Feliz at eight.

"Yeah, I've been thinking about it," I said. I pulled my coat around me a little tighter—Bay Area winters can get really chilly. And I was wearing a cute first-date outfit, which was obviously stupid in this weather, especially since I was hiding it all anyway under this big, lunky parka. "I don't know," I went on. "It's just that I don't have any desire to be in college right now. I mean, I've spent my whole life in this city. I've barely traveled anywhere else, and I don't want to just go plop myself down somewhere for another four years of school. I should go see more of the world first, I think."

Rex squinted and looked off into the distance, as if the answer was floating somewhere above the Shell gas station on the next block. "Yeah, that makes total sense," he said slowly. "There's no need to follow the crowd just because they're all jumping through hoops."

"No, I guess not." I laughed, "Of course, that's usually how I operate. I just watch what everyone else is doing and then I end up going in totally the opposite direction." Was this what I'd been so worried about? But this was so easy. . . .

Rex turned his cute little squint in my direction. "Yeah," he said. "Walter mentioned you were like that."

I snorted. "Don't believe anything he tells you about me! I mean, Walter used to eat paste all the way up until fifth grade. In fact, I think he still does. His breath always smells kind of funny after art class."

He laughed and said, "Naw, I think he appreciates it." He smiled that crooked little smile at me. "I, for one, think being contrary is a wonderful quality in a girl."

Just then the big, goateed bouncer opened the doors and the crowd of hipsters started clambering to get in. "Come on," Rex said, grabbing my hand. "We want to get right up front." We pushed our way inside and I thought my hand might melt from sheer, total giddiness.

* * * * *

WORDS ABOUT EXPLORATION AND ESCAPE

I've lived in the Bay Area my whole life—I'd like to be **transient**, just for once.
 transient (*adj*): moving around a lot

RELATED WORDS

Growing up, my dad was a **nomad**; he never lived in one place longer than a few years.
 nomad (*n*): person who moves constantly from place to place, with no fixed home

When I go hiking, I take only the most **utilitarian** things.
 utilitarian (*adj*): designed more to be practical than beautiful

I'd like to go someplace **precarious**—I need to break out of my safety net.
 precarious (*adj*): dangerous and unstable

My dad doesn't believe I have the **temerity** to put myself in **jeopardy** like that.
> **temerity** (*n*): reckless confidence
> **jeopardy** (*n*): danger

I'd like to travel and pretend I'm a **fugitive**, making up new names for myself in each city.
> **fugitive** (*n*): someone who is escaping the law

I'd like to visit all the places where the Chinese **diaspora** has spread to—Taiwan, Hong Kong, Singapore, etc.
> **diaspora** (*n*): an ethnic or cultural group that is spread out through various parts of the world

Planning an entire year abroad would be a **tedious** but rewarding task.
> **tedious** (*adj*): boring and repetitive

I'd like to visit those parts of the world where westernization hasn't **encroached** entirely.
> **encroach** (*v*): to intrude gradually

Once I mentioned to my dad that I'd like to make an **expedition** to Kenya.
> **expedition** (*n*): a trip made by a group for a specific purpose (to explore, to battle, etc.)

He said I could make an **excursion** to Safeway instead.
> **excursion** (*n*): a short trip to a place and back

When my mom **immigrated** to the United States, she was sad to leave behind her family.
> **immigrate** (*v*): to move to and settle in a new country

When you immigrate to one country, you are always **emigrating** from another.
> **emigrate** (*v*): to leave a country, especially your native one

I hope that spending some time away will allow me to **ruminate** on my way of life.
> **ruminate** (*v*): to think carefully and at length about something

The following words all have to do with thinking and questioning.

I don't have enough time to **contemplate** anything in my day-to-day life. I'd like to spend some time really **delving** into a single topic. All I have to do now is **ascertain** exactly what that "something" should be. I'm not sure yet what my dad thinks about the whole thing. I'm scared to get him to **evince** an opinion. I don't think he'll quite **distinguish** how taking a year off before college isn't the same thing as slacking off for twelve months.

contemplate (*v*): to think carefully

delve (*v*): to dive into; to investigate thoroughly

ascertain (*v*): to decide with certainty

evince (*v*): to show a feeling or characteristic clearly

distinguish (*v*): to tell something apart from something else

I'd like to go somewhere where, for once, Americans are the **alien** presence.

alien (*adj*): foreign

It looks like Janet's and my paths may **diverge** at this point—she will definitely go to college.

diverge (*v*): to split up and go in different directions

I'd like to find a **utopia** out there where no one ever has to make big, important decisions!

utopia (*n*): an ideal, perfect, and harmonious place

As much as I love my family, **proximity** to them isn't a high priority for next year.

proximity (*n*): closeness

I don't know what I'd do if I lived in a foreign country; I suppose I could just move someplace and then **reconnoiter** while I'm there.

reconnoiter (*v*): to explore a place to gather information

Maybe I'll take a year off and **sequester** myself somewhere quiet.

sequester (*v*): to keep in an isolated place

I can **abnegate** television, shopping, and lattes in favor of an **ascetic** lifestyle.

abnegate (*v*): give up something

ascetic (*adj*): living without any worldly possessions and practicing self-denial

WORDS ABOUT MOTION

I hate the fact that people our age feel **propelled** into college.
propel (*v*): to push forward forcefully

Since I drive everywhere, I rarely exercise my **ambulatory** powers.
ambulatory (*adj*): having to do with walking

RELATED WORDS

The following verbs describe all kinds of moving.
circumambulate (*v*): to walk around something
traverse (*v*): to cover a particular amount of space
gallivant (*v*): to travel joyfully
meander (*v*): to move slowly and without purpose
traipse (*v*): to walk casually and heavily
amble (*v*): to walk casually and slowly
careen (*v*): to move at top speed

I'd like to buy one of those multitrip train tickets and just make a **peregrination** around Europe.
peregrination (*n*): a long journey

If I stay here at home, I think I will **stagnate**.
stagnate (*v*): to weaken and become stale from staying in one place

WORDS ABOUT LANDSCAPES

I'd like to stand on a **precipice** and look down into clear, blue water.
precipice (*n*): a high, dangerous rock face

I'd like to get stuck in a **quagmire** and have to be fished out by a donkey.
quagmire (*n*): a sticky, boggy area

TRAVEL AND ADVENTURE

I'd like to visit a seaside city and watch the boats on the **quay**.

> **quay** (*n*): a platform that runs along a harbor, for loading and unloading boats

My friend's older brother spent a year on a farm in Israel and learned all about **agriculture**.

> **agriculture** (*n*): the science of farming

RELATED WORDS

He's now devoted to an **agrarian** lifestyle and lives in a house he built himself. He specifically picked a place with highly **arable** land, so he could produce all his own food.

> **agrarian** (*adj*): having to do with farming and land
> **arable** (*adj*): suitable for farming

The Mojave Desert is extremely **arid**.

> **arid** (*adj*): very dry

Just thinking about it makes me feel **parched**. I need a Gatorade.

> **parched** (*adj*): very dry; very thirsty

Once I tried skydiving, but I'm far too **terrestrial** a person to enjoy that.

> **terrestrial** (*adj*): having to do with the earth

When I asked my brothers where they thought I should go for my year abroad, they answered, "How 'bout someplace **extraterrestrial**." Wiseasses.

> **extraterrestrial** (*adj*): coming from a place other than planet Earth

I've always enjoyed **aerial** photography, but I could never do it myself.

> **aerial** (*adj*): having to do with the air or sky

The vineyard in France was lush and **arboreal**.

> **arboreal** (*adj*): having to do with trees

YOUR TURN

Indicate whether the pairs of words below have similar or different meanings.

1. sequester   hide
2. utilitarian   useful
3. stagnate   propel
4. contemplate   circumambulate
5. parched   arid
6. delve   explore
7. arable   aerial
8. diverge   separate
9. tedious   precarious
10. excursion   trip

In each of the groups below, choose the word that does not belong.

11. ruminate   contemplate   reflect   traverse
12. amble   agitate   traipse   meander
13. precariousness   jeopardy   nomad   danger

Choose the word that best completes the sentence.

14. I was scared to jump off the _____ diving board.
    (A) alien (B) parched (C) precipitous (D) fugitive

15. When the prisoner escaped, he had to live as a(n) _____, in constant fear of capture.
    (A) ascetic (B) alien (C) nomad (D) fugitive

16. Janet and I spent a lazy Sunday _____ through the mall.
    (A) meandering (B) diverging (C) emigrating (D) encroaching

17. The land here is quite _____ and suitable for farming.
    (A) arid (B) parched (C) arable (D) aerial

TRAVEL AND ADVENTURE

18. I was given the _____ task of cataloguing all our old family photos—twelve boxes in all.

    (A) arable (B) onerous (C) precarious (D) terrestrial

19. My friend Jim studies _____ geography. Right now, he's studying land formations on Mars.

    (A) ascetic (B) utilitarian (C) extraterrestrial (D) arid

20. When you watch a movie on TV, they always put the commercial right at the moment of greatest _____ to keep you hooked.

    (A) abnegation (B) stagnation (C) arboreal (D) jeopardy

21. Rex set off on a lonely _____ through the woods, making sure to wear sturdy shoes.

    (A) peregrination (B) abnegation (C) emigration (D) quagmire

22. Many members of the Indian _____ live in Canada, Africa, and the United States.

    (A) agriculture (B) diaspora (C) utilitarian (D) expedition

23. When my brothers were little, babysitters had a hard time _____ one from the other.

    (A) ambling (B) diverging (C) delving (D) distinguishing

24. Mike _____ Wayne off the roof and onto the trampoline.

    (A) encroached (B) traipsed (C) ruminated (D) propelled

25. When I saw the kid next to me cheating on the math test, I was stuck in a moral _____. I didn't know if it would be better to tell someone or keep it to myself and let the teacher catch it.

    (A) ascetic (B) quagmire (C) quay (D) peregrination

TRAVEL AND ADVENTURE

CHAPTER 14
HOW TO TALK ABOUT SICKNESS AND HORROR MOVIES

Janet was at my house for one of our marathon horror-movie nights. Tonight's theme was evil zombies and we were watching *28 Days Later*, which is about this crazy virus that turns the population of London into a bunch of nasty, vomiting apelike people. It's a good thing my brothers weren't around tonight—this movie would have given them *way* too many ideas. Come to think of it, they already resemble nasty, vomiting apelike people plenty enough as it is.

Janet was getting over the flu, so she was curled up on the couch with a bowl of soup. She kept blowing her nose with these big, honking noises that, if she weren't my best friend, would have totally grossed me out. "You better not finish those Kleenex, because I don't have anymore. You'll just have to use your sleeves."

"Thanks, Alex, I appreciate that," she replied. Only it sounded more like, "Dags, Alex. I abbresh' dat."

I waited until she blew her nose again—the loudest one yet—before I asked, "So, you've worked it all out with Andrew?"

"Yup," she replied, crumpling up her tissue. "Done and done." In the past few weeks, Rex and I had gone out a few more times, and talked on the phone for what seemed like a million hours. So I decided I was going to ask him to the Winter Ball. Normally, I hate stuff like that; it gives me a rash. But Janet had been working so hard on it and had even arranged for Tom the DJ to spin instead of the lame guy the school normally gets. So I agreed. I was even getting a little excited—but if you quote me on it, I'll deny it. The plan we'd come up with was to pretend I was writing a feature on local bands for the *Tatler*, and during the interview I'd ask Rex to go with me. I figured, if I was going to ask a guy to a formal, I should at least do something cool with it. Janet had gotten Andrew, the music editor, to call the Giants up to arrange it all.

135

My dad wandered into the room at that point and stared at the TV for a minute. "Reminds me of Mike and Wayne," he said at last. "Alex, these came for you in the mail." He passed me a bunch of large envelopes, which I tore open. They were the travel brochures I'd requested. Mexico, China, Nepal . . . I flipped through them excitedly before passing them to Janet. "What are these for?" my dad asked cautiously. "Some kind of school project?"

"No, Dad," I said breathlessly. "I think I might do some traveling."

"After college? Sure, that might be a good idea."

"No, Dad—I mean next year. Maybe instead of college. Or before college, at least."

My dad's face turned a shade of purple unknown to Crayola. "Totally out of the question!" he said. "You'll be going to college next year and that's final. End of discussion." He looked at Janet and then thought better about getting into a fight at that moment. "You talk some sense into her, Janet. I'm going to bed. We'll talk about this tomorrow."

Ugh. I'd rather meet a flesh-eating zombie than have *that* conversation.

* * * * *

WORDS ABOUT BEING ILL

This was a really **inopportune** moment for Janet to fall sick, because she had a big debate tournament this weekend.

inopportune (*adj*): coming at a bad time

She had lost her voice for three days, and she was worried it had **atrophied**.

atrophy (*v*): to weaken from disuse

RELATED WORDS

The flu had **debilitated** her, and her strength and energy had suffered a
diminution.

> **debilitate** (*v*): to weaken
> **diminution** (*n*): a shrinking or reduction

Two days earlier, she had been in **abject** misery.

> **abject** (*adj*): no hope of relief

She must have caught a **contagion** from school. People were dropping like flies
from the flu that week.

> **contagion** (*n*): an illness that spreads from one person to another

Janet's totally self-conscious about her dry elbows, so she always carries
emollient.

> **emollient** (*n*): a cream

She also carries an **unguent** for her chapped lips.

> **unguent** (*n*): a healing ointment

Janet had been feeling gross for a while; it took her a few days to get the **malaise**
diagnosed as the flu.

> **malaise** (*n*): a general feeling of sickness. The word can also refer to a
> general feeling of dissatisfaction or worry: "My brothers were suffering
> from some kind of *malaise*, but they just said it was the blues."

I should have taken the hint and gone to the doctor to get **inoculated** against the
flu, but I never bothered.

> **inoculate** (*v*): to make immune to a disease

I'm not very knowledgeable about **pathology**; I guess I just figured I wouldn't
catch the flu if I just concentrated really hard on staying healthy.

> **pathology** (*n*): the study of diseases

Janet was **recuperating** nicely—it didn't stick around too long.

> **recuperate** (*v*): to recover from illness or injury

The pain and fever had **abated**.

> **abate** (*v*): to ease, to lessen

A synonym for *abate* is **subside** (*v*): to become less active or intense.

SICKNESS AND HORROR

Yesterday, though, she had looked totally **decrepit**, so we postponed our movie marathon and I made her go home to take a bubble bath.

>**decrepit** (*adj*): old and worn out

WORDS ABOUT PLANNING

Janet and I had been **formulating** the plan for days.

>**formulate** (*v*): to plan carefully and in detail

She was my primary **accomplice** in the whole thing.

>**accomplice** (*n*): someone who knowingly helps another person commit a crime

RELATED WORDS

Janet will always be there to **abet** me during any of my crazy schemes.

>**abet** (*v*): to help someone, especially in doing something illegal

The day before the plan went down, I was **fraught** with tension.

>**fraught** (*adj*): full of nervous anxiety; filled with dangers or complications

It was a **momentous** occasion—this was the day I was finally going to let Rex know I really liked him.

>**momentous** (*adj*): extremely important, especially in terms of its effect on future events

We tried to be very **clandestine** about the planning—we didn't want my nosy brothers to find out anything.

>**clandestine** (*adj*): secret, often illegal

I can always trust Janet to be **discreet** about these things. She's got a mouth like a steel trap. And you've got to be really **surreptitious** around my brothers— they're always **conniving** something or other, and they can sniff out another plot a mile away.

>**discreet** (*adj*): done without being noticed; modest
>**surreptitious** (*adj*): done sneakily
>**connive** (*v*): to secretly plot to do something, usually something illegal

Janet came up with the **machination** of having me write a "special report" on the local indie music scene.

> **machination** (*n*): a cunning or complicated plot designed to achieve something particular

It was, of course, just a **contrivance** to get me to a band rehearsal. If Rex saw through the **ruse**, he was very polite about it.

> **contrivance** (*n*): something cunning done to accomplish something
> **ruse** (*n*): a trick designed to fool someone

WORDS ABOUT HORROR MOVIES

I love a good horror movie—the **gorier**, the better. In my opinion, a horror movie isn't worth my time unless I see at least a dozen bodies wallowing in blood.

> **gory** (*adj*): disgusting, bloody

RELATED WORDS

Gruesome (*adj*))and **grisly** (*adj*))are synonyms for *gory*.

Janet shares my love of **macabre** stories—underneath that sunny exterior is a really twisted girl! We especially like movies that expose the **sordid** side of everyday life. Our movie marathons are not for the **squeamish**.

> **macabre** (*adj*): including dark, horrific elements and concerned with themes of death
> **sordid** (*adj*): dirty, depressing
> **squeamish** (*adj*): easily disgusted or shocked

In this movie, the hero manages to off one zombie by **defenestration**.

> **defenestration** (*n*): throwing someone out of a window

These words all describe ways of killing people.

> **disarticulation** (*n*): separating at the joints
>
> **decapitation** (*n*): cutting someone's head off
>
> **dismemberment** (*n*): cutting someone's limbs off, tearing into pieces

It was pretty disgusting, though, when the zombies started **gorging** themselves on dead bodies.

> **gorge** (*v*): to greedily eat excessive amounts of something

These words have to do with eating.

What would happen if you were a vegetarian zombie and couldn't deal with being **carnivorous**, let alone being **cannibalistic**?

> **carnivorous** (*adj*): eating meat
>
> **cannibal** (*n*): a human who eats other human beings

That night, I knew I was going to dream about **carcasses** walking around my house.

> **carcass** (*n*): dead body

Personally, I like my dead bodies **supine** and suffering from a bad case of **rigor mortis**.

> **supine** (*adj*): lying on the back
>
> **rigor mortis** (*n*): when a dead body goes stiff

I also like werewolf movies, particularly *Teen Wolf*. Michael J. Fox, in my opinion, is way cuter in his **lupine** form.

> **lupine** (*adj*): having to do with wolves

Despite my love of movies with lots of bloody effects, I still can't manage getting **sanguinary** tests done at the doctor's office.

> **sanguinary** (*adj*): having to do with blood

YOUR TURN

Match the vocab words on the left with the word or phrase that means the opposite on the right.

1.	carcass	a.	open
2.	squeamish	b.	get sicker
3.	surreptitious	c.	pleasant
4.	inopportune	d.	tough
5.	recuperate	e.	unimportant
6.	decrepit	f.	uncomplicated
7.	momentous	g.	live human being
8.	gruesome	h.	hopeful, optimistic
9.	abject	i.	well-timed
10.	fraught	j.	healthy

In each of the groups below, choose the word that does not belong.

11. diminish   strengthen   atrophy   debilitate
12. open   secret   clandestine   surreptitious
13. defenestration   decapitation   demonstration   disarticulation
14. gory   gruesome   gorging   macabre
15. machination   chance   contrivance   plot

SICKNESS AND HORROR

Choose the best word from the list given below to fill in the blanks. Not every word will be used.

abate   accomplice   ruse   unguent   cannibal   candestine   supine   connive   inoculation   malaise   sordid   lupine   gorge   defenestration

16. My dad insisted I get a flu _____ after Janet fell sick.
17. Janet's symptoms will _____ after a few days of bed rest and chicken soup.
18. Mike is Wayne's permanent _____. They are always helping each other get up to no good.

19. Romeo and Juliet had to have _____ meetings because their families hated each other.

20. It seemed like the magician made an elephant disappear, but it was just a(n) _____ accomplished with smoke and mirrors.

21. I was suffering from _____ last month. I didn't want to get out of bed, I felt so depressed.

22. Chapstick is a great _____ for chapped lips.

23. There were rows of people lying _____ on the beach, trying to soak up some sun.

24. The man in Germany was charged with being a(n) _____, but he claimed the victim wanted to be eaten.

25. I don't like watching the news—all the _____ stories upset me.

HAPTER 1
HOW TO TALK ABOUT A BROKEN HEART

That weekend, I found myself sitting in a big garage watching the Giants put away their instruments. I had watched the last half hour of their rehearsal, which was awesome—as usual. Sometimes I have fantasies of working as a reporter for *Spin* or *Rolling Stone* and traveling with grimy, up-and-coming bands as they tour the continental United States in a nasty bus waiting for their big break. And then I'd write an amazing, sensitive article about them and they'd become famous and dedicate every album after that to me and put little pictures of me in their liner notes.

Hey, it could happen. Haven't you seen *Almost Famous*?

Anyway, as the rest of the band started packing up all the equipment, Rex came and sat down to be interviewed. "Okay," I said, trying to look official. "First question. When did you guys get together as a band?"

Rex pushed the floppy hair out of his eyes. "About a year ago. Melissa and I played drums and guitar in another band, the Sabotages. When they broke up, we picked up Don, Mick and Rudy and started the Giants. Actually, you want to know a dirty little secret?" Rex leaned into the tape recorder and lowered his voice. "We all met in junior high, at state band camp. But don't put that in your article—it's not very rock and roll of us."

I promised it would remain confidential, and moved on to my next question. "What are your influences?"

He thought for a moment. "Well, we love stuff like Sonic Youth, Elvis Costello, the Strokes . . . but lately we've been trying to experiment more with soul music. Lyrically, we just write about whatever we're thinking about. Girls, usually," he grinned. "But we all share the writing responsibilities, which keeps things varied."

Gulp. Time for the big plunge. Here goes. "Okay, final question. . . ." I tried to keep my voice steady, but somehow it ended up coming out as one long word: "Willyougotothewinterformalwithme?"

The rest of the band looked at me, then looked at Rex, and burst out laughing. Melissa—a girl I had thought was cool until this very second—laughed so hard I thought her nose ring was going to pop out. Don made a big show of putting his hands on his knees and trying to catch his breath, while Rudy wiped tears of laughter from his eyes. "Yeah, Rex at a formal," gasped Melissa. "Real likely!" Then they headed inside the house, laughing and slapping one another on the backs all the way.

I was totally, utterly, completely mortified. Rex was laughing too and saying something like, "Yeah, I'm not really into that kind of thing," but I didn't hear him because I was already running out the door.

*   *   *   *   *

WORDS ABOUT DESTRUCTION

When Rex laughed like that with his friends, I felt like I had been **annihilated**.
   annihilate (*v*): to ruin completely

RELATED WORDS

These are some other words related to destruction.

My already low self-confidence was **razed** to the ground. My heart was **decimated** and **obliterated.** I felt like it had had all the blood drained out of it, leaving it a **desiccated** and withered thing. Over the next few days, just thinking about my humiliation would make my heart **corrode** even further. I had just sunk into the depths of social **perdition**.

   raze (*v*): to bring a structure down to the ground
   decimated (*adj*): completely ruined
   obliterated (*adj*): destroyed without a trace
   desiccated (*adj*): dried out
   corrode (*v*): to wear away, as if with acid or chemicals
   perdition (*n*): complete ruin

Honestly, I've been **buffeted** by love so often, I'm amazed I haven't given up yet.
   buffet (*v*): to hit something hard and repeatedly

My ego can't take all this **battery**. I feel like I've been **bludgeoned** by a sledgehammer.

>**battery** (*n*): an unlawful physical assault
>
>**bludgeon** (*v*): to hit hard with a blunt object

Inside I was in **chaos**, but on the outside I was as smooth as butter.

>**chaos** (*n*): state of complete disorder

I thought about all the **carnage** I saw in those zombie movies, and I thought I'd rather be one of those guys than me right now.

>**carnage** (*n*): widespread killing and slaughter

WORDS ABOUT SURPRISE AND EMBARRASSMENT

I was totally **flabbergasted** by Rex's response. I totally thought he liked me.

>**flabbergasted** (*adj*): bewildered, totally amazed

RELATED WORDS

Two synonyms for *flabbergasted* are **nonplussed** (*adj*) and **baffled** (*adj*).

I just couldn't **fathom** it at first.

>**fathom** (*v*): to understand something, particularly something complex or mystical

I was so sure he **reciprocated** my feelings.

>**reciprocate** (*v*): to return, to respond in kind

I managed to maintain my **composure** till I left, though.

>**composure** (*n*): calmness; control over one's emotions

It started so well, but the whole thing was such a **debacle**, I can't even bring myself to think about it.

>**debacle** (*n*): when something goes horribly wrong

Walter Chen **accosted** me in the hall to find out more about the event.
> **accost** (*v*): to aggressively stop someone in order to speak to him or her

At the moment it happened, I was in a total state of **discomfiture**—I was so embarrassed, I didn't know what to do with myself.
> **discomfiture** (*n*): confusion and embarrassment

After a while, though, the painful **mortification** faded to a general sense of **chagrin**.
> **mortification** (*n*): total humiliation
> **chagrin** (*n*): feeling of frustration or shame due to disappointment (a milder term than something like *mortification* or *humiliation*)

I was convinced the **stigma** of it all would stick to me forever, and I'd always be remembered as "that girl who got shot down."
> **stigma** (*n*): a bad mark on someone's reputation

Even though I was sure people had heard the story, no one at school treated me with any **derision** after it happened. I guess all that **ignominy** was just in my head.
> **derision** (*n*): scorn, ridicule
> **ignominy** (*n*): great personal disgrace, dishonor

I mean, it wasn't like people were **disseminating** the story on the stalls of the girls' room.
> **disseminate** (*v*): to spread (usually referring to information)

Though I thought about writing my own little **obloquy** about Rex in there.
> **obloquy** (*n*): an abusive verbal attack

I guess everyone has to deal with this kind of **indignity** at some point in her romantic career.
> **indignity** (*n*): something that offends one's dignity or self-esteem

I felt really **slighted** by Rex—I thought we had a deeper relationship than that.
> **slight** (*v*): to insult someone, especially in a way that involves ignoring or overlooking the person

WORDS ABOUT HEARTBREAK

There was no way I was going to **abase** myself in front of a boy.

abase (*v*): to degrade someone; to make someone feel horrible and small

My dad asked—loudly and inconsiderately—why I kept moping around the house and looking so **despondent**.

despondent (*adj*): completely unhappy

RELATED WORDS

Some more fun words about emotional pain.

I told him I was in **anguish**, and he shouldn't bother trying to talk me out of it, because I was totally **inconsolable**. I spent all my time wandering around my room, which seemed totally **desolate** and boring now. I think my dad knew I was **aggrieved** about a boy, but he didn't push the subject.

anguish (*n*): extreme pain

inconsolable (*adj*): so deeply sad that you can't be comforted

desolate (*adj*): sad, empty, gloomy

aggrieved (*adj*): bothered because of having been treated badly

No doubt my dad would say this kind of **tribulation** was good for my character.

tribulation (*n*): a great difficulty

Boys seem so sweet and cuddly, but they're really evil, **treacherous** creatures that are not to be trusted.

treacherous (*adj*): dangerous; betraying

I think I hit my **nadir** that day.

nadir (*n*): the absolute bottom

The antonym for **nadir** is **acme** (*n*): the absolute peak.

Janet bought me a huge Starbucks frappucino to **alleviate** my pain.

alleviate (*v*): to provide relief

It's amazing how expensive coffee drinks can act like an emotional **analgesic**. We joked that I needed a shot of **anesthesia** in my heart.

> **analgesic** (*n*): a kind of medication, like aspirin, that relieves pain without putting you to sleep
>
> **anesthesia** (*n*): something that deadens feeling so as to relieve pain

Oh well, crushes are **ephemeral** when you're my age. I'll probably get over it soon.

> **ephemeral** (*adj*): short-lived

My affections are usually pretty **mercurial**—take my short-lived love affair with the Backstreet Boys, for example.

> **mercurial** (*adj*): quick and changeable in temperament

I **abhorred** the thought of seeing Rex after that.

> **abhor** (*v*): to hate

He became an **anathema** to me.

> **anathema** (*n*): something that is hated

Janet swore she'd **avenge** me by publishing a nasty review of their next live show in the *Tatler*.

> **avenge** (*v*): to take revenge on someone else's behalf

I'll still **cherish** the memory of the poetry reading, though.

> **cherish** (*v*): to adore, to treat as a precious object

If I ever saw him at the Cup or anywhere else, I planned on seeking **asylum** in the girls' room.

> **asylum** (*n*): a place where one can escape punishment or seek safety

That's it—I'm **renouncing** boys forever.

> **renounce** (*v*): to formally give up something

YOUR TURN

Indicate whether the pairs of words below have similar or different meanings.

1. buffet   bludgeon
2. discomfiture   chagrin
3. accost   comfort
4. nadir   acme
5. abhor   adore
6. alleviate   mitigate
7. ephemeral   long-lasting
8. cherish   renounce
9. despondency   anguish
10. obloquy   praise

From the list below, select the word that best describes each person portrayed in the phrases that follow.

desolate   composed   mortified   mercurial   flabbergasted   treacherous

11. Someone sighing and looking sad on a park bench
12. Someone who just saw an elephant fall out of a city window
13. Someone waiting around the corner with a knife
14. Someone who doesn't get upset when his dad yells at him
15. Someone who is caught walking out of the bathroom with his fly unzipped
16. Someone who decides he loves rap one day, country the next, and classical music the next

Choose the word that best completes the sentence.

17. The Spice Girls' fame was _____. What happened to them, anyway?
    (A) treacherous (B) inconsolable (C) ephemeral (D) bludgeoned

18. My room is always in a state of _____. I'm amazed I can find anything in it.

    (A) stigma (B) chaos (C) derision (D) obloquy

19. When my old lab partner walked by me in the hall without even saying hi, I felt totally _____.

    (A) accosted (B) reciprocated (C) alleviated (D) slighted

20. I _____ broccoli. I'd rather eat cafeteria burritos!

    (A) abase (B) disseminate (C) mortify (D) abhor

21. I was _____ after the Rex debacle. Not even Janet could cheer me up.

    (A) inconsolable (B) mercurial (C) accosted (D) obliterated

22. I couldn't possibly _____ calculus. I can barely make it through pre-algebra.

    (A) buffet (B) raze (C) deride (D) fathom

23. After Walter wet the bed once at sleepaway camp, he had to endure the _____ of being known as a bed wetter.

    (A) carnage (B) dissemination (C) stigma (D) composure

24. I was completely _____ when I saw Madonna at the mall last weekend.

    (A) reciprocated (B) obliterated (C) nonplussed (D) aggrieved

25. A boring desk job would be _____ to me. I want a job that will keep me really active.

    (A) mercurial (B) anathema (C) cherished (D) asylum

CHAPTER 16
MISLEADING WORDS

Fabulous. Just perfect. Now my dad and Rex *both* think I'm a loser. How could I have been so stupid? Didn't I know that guys lied? Especially teenage guys? Especially teenage *musician* guys?

I was sitting in my room with the door locked. A pile of Angry Girl CDs was lying by my stereo. Janet and I had picked them out last night, figuring that I would need at least a week's supply to live down the awful interview incident. "I can't *believe* that happened," she had said, passing me her old Alanis Morissette album. "I mean, for weeks things are going well and then, poof! I can't believe he didn't stop his friends from laughing, at least."

"I *know*," I said, taking another heaping spoonful of Ben and Jerry's Chunky Monkey. "Tell me about it. I just can't believe he pulled such a 180 on me. Why do boys always say one thing and then do another?" I put in Alanis and let her loud, whiny voice wash over me. "Whatever. I'm over it." Janet said that was a good attitude to have.

I was tired of being cranky and lame. I decided to do something about it, so I got to work on some new poems. So far in the Angry Girl CD list I had gone through Bjork, Liz Phair, and Sleater-Kinney, and now I was listening to the Donnas as loud as possible (but not *too* loud—the last thing I wanted to deal with was my dad yelling at me about my music). The phone rang just as I was getting through a really good sonnet. Probably Janet, offering me some more moral support. "Hi darling," I said.

An unmistakable voice on the other line barked, "So, do you want to go to the formal or not?"

"*Wal*ter? Walter Chen?" I couldn't believe it. "What kind of stupid trick are you pulling?" God! Had he *no* sense of decency? I was even less of a fan of Walter's today, since he was cousins with That Boy Who Shall Remain Nameless.

"No trick," Walter said. "My cousin was a jackass for pulling that on you. And . . ." he stammered. "And he doesn't deserve you, okay?"

I was floored. Did Walter Chen have a soul after all?

"So, stop being a moron, Lee, and say you'll go to formal with me."

Well, nice to know some things never change.

"Walter, I'd be happy to go." Wait a minute, what was I saying?! Oh well, too late. "After all, I wouldn't want my dress to go to waste. But you do realize, Walter, that this is not some Freddie Prinze, Jr. movie—*nothing* is going to happen between us at this dance. You got that?"

Walter laughed. "Deal, Lee. I wouldn't want your cooties all over me anyway. Just manage to dress like a normal person, okay?"

"Will do, Walter," I said as we hung up.

Jesus. If live to be a hundred, I will *never* understand boys.

*   *   *   *   *

So, in honor of all the **duplicitous** (*adj*) boys out there (in other words, all the deceptive, misleading boys), I've put together a list of words that don't mean what they sound like, or words that sound like other words. Take **pulchritude** (*n*) for example. Who would have ever guessed that word meant "beauty"? Doesn't it sound like something you'd use to clean your drain with? So here goes. Use some of them in casual conversation and watch your friends get all confused. (Try *logorrhea*, another old favorite!)

*   *   *   *   *

MISLEADING WORDS

I like watching little kids at the playground. They run around from place to place in such a funny, **apian** manner.

> **apian** (*adj*): having to do with bees (not apes, surprisingly enough)

My father was completely **apoplectic** when I said I wanted to take a year off to travel.

> **apoplectic** (*adj*): really angry

At MFC, the creation of perfect ice-cream Squashies is my **bailiwick**.

> **bailiwick** (*n*): an area in which a person has a special ability or responsibility (not something that gave you nightmares as a little kid)

Whenever I get a box of original Krispy Kremes, I get an even **baker's dozen**.
   baker's dozen (*n*): A baker's dozen isn't a dozen at all—the phrase means "a set of thirteen."

My idea of **beatitude** is a world without lame teenage boys.
   beatitude (*n*): perfect happiness and peace

In English class, Walter Chen is always making loud, **bumptious** arguments.
   bumptious (*adj*): aggressively opinionated

My cousin has a **congenital** heart defect that keeps her in and out of the hospital.
   congenital (*adj*): Nope, not something you can catch from a toilet seat. *Congenital* describes a condition that has existed since birth.

Janet's favorite touch at the Winter Formal was the disco ball, which **coruscated** as it spun.
   coruscate (*v*): to shine, to flash brightly

When it came to eating, my brothers' **cupidity** is alarming. When you see them at the dinner table, you'd think they'd been starved for weeks.
   cupidity (*n*): greed

Watching the *Buffy* marathon last weekend **enervated** me—after ten hours of lying on my couch, I barely had the energy to get up and go to bed.
   enervate (*v*): to weaken

Walter and I are always getting into **frays** in English class.
   fray (*n*): as a verb, it means "to shred something"; as a noun, though, it means "a fight."

After a few weeks, the chocolate bar I left on my desk dried up and became **friable**.
   friable (*adj*): easily broken up into little pieces

When Walter wants to wheedle an A out of a teacher, he gets this **fulsome** tone in his voice that I hate.
   fulsome (*adj*): offensively fawning

When my dad asked me why I was being so mopey, I just **hedged** the question.
   hedge (*v*): to avoid answering a question directly

I envy girls with **helicoid** hair—mine is stick straight.
> **helicoid** (*adj*): shaped like a spiral

They're cutting back my hours at MFC, so I'm going to have to **husband** my money if I want to go to that White Stripes concert in March.
> **husband** (*v*): No, I don't mean I'm going to try to marry a rich guy. To *husband* means to use something economically.

My brothers are **immutable** in the fact that they're never mute.
> **immutable** (*adj*): unchangeable

My father's resolve is **impregnable**—I don't think there's any way I can convince him that he's wrong.
> **impregnable** (*adj*): unable to be broken by an outside force

Christina Aguilera is **infamous** for wearing awful outfits.
> **infamous** (*adj*): This word doesn't mean "not famous"—the word describes someone famous for a bad reputation.

When Rex turned me down for the Winter Formal, it broke my heart into **infinitesimal** pieces.
> **infinitesimal** (*adj*): This isn't a synonym for *infinite*—it means "very, very tiny."

Janet was **instrumental** in making me feel better.
> **instrumental** (*adj*): necessary in order to bring something about

At first I thought my grief would be **insuperable**.
> **insuperable** (*adj*): unable to be overcome or gotten rid of

Sometimes my jock brothers are quite **jocular**, especially when they sense I'm in a really bad mood.
> **jocular** (*adj*): joking, playful

Even though they're cousins, Walter and Rex couldn't be more different. If you **juxtaposed** them, though, you might get a pretty neat guy—smart and cool, but probably still crazy.
> **juxtapose** (*v*): to put two (usually unlike) things together

When I get my heart broken by a boy, I just want to lie on the couch and watch **lachrymose** movies all day.
> **lachrymose** (*adj*): crying easily, or making someone else cry

The head cheerleader at our high school suffers from **logorrhea**. It's sad, really.
logorrhea (*n*): extreme talkativeness. It usually also implies incoherence, as in someone with a mental disease.

Janet needed to **marshal** some people to help with Winter Formal setup, but I managed to duck out of it.
marshal (*v*): to gather people together and organize them

I hate watching my brothers **masticate** at the dinner table.
masticate (*v*): Ew! Get your mind out of the gutter. It means "to grind with the teeth."

Noisome smells are always coming from my brothers' room.
noisome (*adj*): offensive to the senses

When all of Rex's friends laughed at me, I felt completely **nugatory**.
nugatory (*adj*): completely unimportant

If you put a plastic cup in the microwave, it becomes **plastic**.
plastic (*adj*): easily bent and shaped

I should have known the idea of dating an indie rock boy was a **quixotic** fantasy.
quixotic (*adj*): overly idealistic, romanticized and impractical (This word is drawn from the title character of Miguel Cervantes's novel *Don Quixote*, about a knight who had these qualities.)

Janet bought a pretty **racy** dress for the Winter Formal—there's going to be a lot of skin exposed.
racy (*adj*): shockingly sexual

When her mom saw it, she said, "Is that a **rent** in your dress, or did it come that way?"
rent (*n*): It can be something you pay a landlord, but here it means "a rip" or "a tear."

When my brothers get grounded, they usually get so **restive** that my dad goes crazy and lets them out early.
restive (*adj*): active and out-of-control

When Janet was sick, she got all **rheumy** and disgusting.
rheumy (*adj*): Nope, your mom's SUV isn't *rheumy*. *Rheum* is a watery discharge coming out of the eyes, nose, or mouth.

Janet lent me a Celine Dion CD, but I find her music so **saccharine**.
    saccharine (*adj*): sickeningly sweet

After the awful incident at the rehearsal, Janet brought me lots of Ben and Jerry's, which had a **salubrious** effect.
    salubrious (*adj*): being good for your health or general well-being

I got a splinter the other day and **scarified** myself trying to get it out.
    scarify (*v*): to scratch the skin

My dad doesn't like the Tin Cup because he thinks it's **seamy**.
    seamy (*adj*): distasteful because of its immorality

I always tell him that, just because it looks **seedy**, that doesn't mean it's filled with bad people.
    seedy (*adj*): Nope, you won't get a tree if you plant something *seedy*. It means "cheap" and "run-down."

When my brothers were little, they used to **somnambulate**. Sometimes they'd do it at the same time and really freak out my parents.
    somnambulate (*v*): to sleepwalk (Actually, this word makes sense if you know the roots—*somni* means "sleep," and *ambulate* means "to walk.")

My dad hoped that getting a job at MFC would teach me the value of money and how to be less **spendthrift**.
    spendthrift (*adj*): Sounds like being "spendthrift" would be a good thing, right? Actually, it doesn't mean "being thrifty," it means the exact opposite—"spending money wastefully and unnecessarily."

After being humiliated, I spent a few days shut up in my room. But then I decided that was lame, so I **spruced** myself up and went out.
    spruce (*v*): to make something look better

Lately, I've been thinking that I'd like to spend next year in the **Strait** of Gibraltar area—Morocco, Spain, and the Mediterranean.
    strait (*n*): a narrow band of water that joins two larger bodies of water

I can't believe Rex dissed me so **summarily**.
    summarily (*adv*): brusquely, rudely, without discussion

Last month, this total **tyro** came swaggering into the Tin Cup and wanted to read his poems. He was so proud of them, but they were really awful.
    tyro (*n*): a complete, rank amateur

I keep **waffling** about whether or not to call him, but Janet keeps convincing me to wait.

> **waffle** (*v*): as a noun, it means something that tastes good with syrup. As a verb, though, it means "to keep changing your opinion."

YOUR TURN

Match the vocab words on the left with their definitions on the right.

1.	bailiwick	a.	easily breakable
2.	congenital	b.	playful, lively
3.	fulsome	c.	seedy
4.	noisome	d.	overly flattering
5.	friable	e.	sleepwalk
6.	insuperable	f.	thin stretch of water
7.	jocular	g.	area of expertise
8.	plastic	h.	flexible
9.	seamy	i.	offensive to the senses
10.	somnambulate	j.	clean up
11.	spruce	k.	unbeatable
12.	strait	l.	existing since birth

Choose the best word from the list given below to fill in the blanks. Not every word will be used.

bumptious   apoplectic   salubrious   apian   spendthrift   lachrymose
logorrhea   juxtapose   tyro   cupidity   rheumy   infamous   quixotic
pulchritude   rent   restive   seamy   nugatory   marshal

13. I tried to sneak through the barbed-wire fence, which left a(n) _____ in my jeans.

14. When he's in a bad mood, my dad loves to watch _____ movies and have himself a good cry.

15. Our neighbors have a flat-screen TV, two new Corvettes, and three expensive computers. Their _____ amazes me.

16. The Miss America pageant is always a major display of _____.

17. The _____ senator liked to argue with people just for the sake of arguing.

18. Bonnie and Clyde were _____ criminals.

19. My piano teacher used to suffer from a bad case of _____. I could never get a word in edgewise.

20. Sadly, her efforts to make me a piano genius were _____ at best. I've never had much musical ability.

21. When our rabbit got sick, her eyes got all _____ and had to be rinsed with water.

22. We used to feed her vitamins, fresh vegetables, and other things that were _____ for her health.

23. Despite being a tennis _____, Mike picked up the sport surprisingly fast.

24. My dad hoped that getting a job would teach me the value of money and cure my _____ ways.

25. When I get sick, I get really _____. I feel so cooped up in the house!

CHAPTER 17
HOW TO TALK ABOUT ARGUMENTS AND RECONCILIATION

The Winter Formal had rolled around, and I was just about to head out the door. Janet had begged me to buy some hideous, pastel-colored thing—"Come *on*, Alex, can't you wear anything besides black?"—but I refused. I was already going to this dance—with Walter Chen, no less—and there was no way I was going to go to it dressed as a cupcake. I had picked out a simple, long black dress, which I was wearing with my trusty old Doc Martens. Just to appease Janet, I wore a little lipstick and put some sparkly clips in my hair.

Too bad I wasn't in a party mood. My dad and I had been fighting all week and I was totally exhausted. Mike and Wayne started off really enjoying it, but soon even *they* got tired of seeing Dad and I go at it every night, and took to eating dinner in their room in protest. Yesterday I got so fed up that I sat down and wrote out a five-page essay on why I should be allowed to go abroad next year. I told him I wanted to see more of the world before I went back to school, and that it would build my character. I told him I wanted to find myself. I was sure it would be no help, but I was just so tired of arguing about it.

I was about to head out the door when my dad came out of his study, holding my essay. "Alex—" he started.

I looked at my watch impatiently. "Dad, I really have to go right now, okay? I have to pick up Walter from his chess tournament and then go to this stupid formal. Can we talk about this tomorrow?"

He looked stern. "No, we can't." Then he took off his glasses and rubbed his eyes. "Alex, you're totally right."

Excuse me?

"I am?" I said.

"Yeah," he said, and sat down on the couch. "I've been pushing this college thing way too hard. This"—he waved my essay—"is pretty good stuff. I forget what a good writer you are." He smiled and then sighed. "Ever since your mom died, I've been pushing you kids pretty hard. Especially you, since those two clowns"— here he gestured up at the twins' room—"are a hopeless case until they finally get over puberty."

"So . . ." I said carefully, "It's okay for me not to go to college next year?"

He sighed again. "Yes, I suppose so. But you have to come up with a detailed plan for me—there's no way I'm just going to buy you a one-way ticket to God-knows-where and leave it at that."

I laughed. "Okay, Dad. I can work with that." I looked at my watch. "Shoot, I really should go get Walter now if I'm going to make this dance."

"Walter? Walter Chen?" Dad looked puzzled. "You mean, that nerd you beat in the spelling bee?"

"Yup, that's the one," I said.

"But I thought you were going out with that hoodlum musician."

"*Dad*," I whined and then blushed. "He's not a hoodlum. And besides, you're not supposed to know about any of that."

Dad grinned. "Alex, you have the loudest phone voice I've ever heard. There's a *lot* I'm not supposed to know about." My mind started racing—did he know about that dirt bike incident? or the time Janet and I cut class to drive to Mexico?—but before I could ask him any questions he was hustling me out the door. "Go pick up your nerd date," he said. "And don't stay out too late!"

* * * * *

WORDS ABOUT ARGUMENTS

Last week, my father launched into a long **tirade** about how not going to college next year would ruin my life.

tirade (*n*): a long outraged speech

RELATED WORDS

These words are all about angry talking.

My father started by **admonishing** me in a kind, fatherly way. When that didn't work, though, he moved on to **chastising** me loudly whenever he could. He kept **carping** on and on about it: at the dinner table, on the way to the supermarket, at the dentist's office. It was all I could do not to hurl **maledictions** at him to match all his **aspersions** of me.

    admonish (*v*): to rebuke, to scold gently

    chastise (*v*): to criticize heavily. *Admonish* is a much milder word than
        chastise.

    carp (*v*): to keep complaining about something

    malediction (*n*): a curse

    aspersion (*n*): criticism

I was in a **quandary**. I really didn't want to be in school next year, but I hated to have my dad so mad at me.

    quandary (*n*): a puzzling situation

The quandary left me **exasperated**.

    exasperated (*adj*): fed up and angry

I had no idea how to **extricate** myself from the situation.

    extricate (*v*): to disentangle oneself from a sticky situation

I was so **disaffected** by the whole thing. Why was my dad acting like such a child?

    disaffected (*adj*): disappointed and dissatisfied

I guess now I know where my brothers get their **pugnacious** attitude.

    pugnacious (*adj*): aggressive

Unluckily for my dad, I was just as **obstinate** as he was, and I wasn't about to just give up.

    obstinate (*adj*): stubborn

I thought I presented a really strong **rationale** in my essay for being allowed to travel.

    rationale (*n*): line of reasoning

WORDS ABOUT MAKING UP

I was really happy when my dad and I **reconciled**—I hate having so much tension in the house!

>   **reconcile** (*v*): to make up. The word can also mean "to accept that something you dislike won't change." As in, "My dad had to *reconcile* himself to the fact that I wasn't going to college next year."

Now our house was in a state of **accord**.

>   **accord** (*n*): agreement; a state of harmony

Dad's apology made me feel **vindicated**.

>   **vindicate** (*v*): to show that someone was justified and correct

Underneath it all, Dad is a really **benevolent** guy who just wants his kids to be happy.

>   **benevolent** (*adj*): kindly

I try to have **compassion** for what he's going through. It's tough to raise three obnoxious teenagers by yourself.

>   **compassion** (*n*): to feel sympathy for another's misfortunes

RELATED WORDS

I'm sure that, once I have kids of my own, I'll really **empathize** with him.

>   **empathize** (*v*): to identify with another person's feelings

My dad was really **contrite** about having been so obdurate.

>   **contrite** (*adj*): genuinely apologetic

Here are some other words about being wrong and being sorry.

I was touched by how **penitent** he was and how badly he wanted to make **amends**. He **expiated** himself by being super-nice to me and barely raising a fuss when I came home from the formal at 3 in the morning. I think he realized that he was just as **culpable** for the fight as I was.

> **penitent** (*adj*): genuinely apologetic
> **amends** (*n*): something done or given to make up for having done wrong
> **expiate** (*v*): to make amends
> **culpable** (*adj*): at fault

Because he was being so reasonable, I **acceded** to his wishes that I come up with a detailed plan for next year.

> **accede** (*v*): to consent to something

At first I did it just to **placate** him, but then I realized that coming up with a plan would be a really good idea.

> **placate** (*v*): to please someone in order to make someone less angry

I **delineated** exactly what my goals were for the year.

> **delineate** (*v*): to explain something in detail

My brothers were amazed at how **docile** I became.

> **docile** (*adj*): meek, easy to control

WORDS ABOUT PROMISES

Dad told me his permission wasn't **unconditional**. I had to take lots of steps to make sure my trip was safe and well-planned.

> **unconditional** (*adj*): guaranteed with no strings attached

His permission would be **tentative** until I came up with a plan.

> **tentative** (*adj*): not definite; likely to change before it is final

He was very **explicit** on that issue.
> **explicit** (*adj*): very clear. The adjective can also mean "very open and direct about sexuality." As in: "My brothers like to hide *explicit* magazines under their beds."

He **stipulated** that I had to go as part of a program, and not on my own.
> **stipulate** (*v*): to specify something as part of an agreement or contract

That was his only **mandate**—other than that, I was free to choose where I wanted to go and what I wanted to do.
> **mandate** (*n*): an official order

I gave him my **assurance** that I would plan it out very carefully.
> **assurance** (*n*): something offered to inspire confidence

We made a **covenant** that he wouldn't micromanage my trip as long as I kept him informed of all my plans.
> **covenant** (*n*): a binding promise or contract

At first I was worried he'd **rescind** his promise, but he didn't.
> **rescind** (*v*): to take back something (like a promise or an argument)

WORDS OF FATHERLY ADVICE

My dad likes giving me advice—he gets a kick out of being all **paternal**.
> **paternal** (*adj*): relating to fathers

RELATED WORDS

> **maternal** (*adj*): relating to mothers
> **fraternal** (*adj*): relating to brothers

There's no corresponding word for "relating to sisters" (sexist, much?) But just like the root *frater* means "brother," *soror* means "sister"—hence the words *fraternity* and *sorority*.

ARGUMENTS

I was glad my dad didn't **interrogate** me about Rex, but maybe I should have asked his advice.

interrogate (*v*): to question aggressively

He's pretty **intuitive** when it comes to guys. I guess it helps that he was one, once.

intuitive (*adj*): known instinctively

I'm sure he would have told me to be **resilient**, and that teenage boys were a dime a dozen.

resilient (*adj*): able to bounce back from hardship

These are some other words Dad likes to use about making it through bad times.

Dad always tells me that **adversity** toughens you up and increases your personal **fortitude**. Handling these things coolly and learning **forbearance** is the first step to becoming an adult (so, he doesn't always follow his own advice . . .).

adversity (*n*): trouble, suffering
fortitude (*n*): strength, stamina
forbearance (*n*): self-control

Dad never wants me to be **submissive** to boys. Submissive to him, yes, but he sees himself as a special exception.

submissive (*adj*): easily giving in

He always wants me to **advocate** for myself—which I think is why he responded so well to that essay.

advocate (*v*): to stand up for something

Dad would tell me to be **objective** about the situation with Rex and think about it unemotionally.

objective (*adj*): without bias or personal involvement

The antonym of *objective* is **subjective** (*adj*): based on opinions and feelings.

If I had decided to stay home from the formal and mope, Dad would have **goaded** me to go.

goad (*v*): to prompt, to provoke

A synonym for *goad* is **exhort** (*v*): to urge someone to do something.

I think that my dad would secretly be very happy if I chose to **forsake** boys forever. Dad doesn't trust most teenage guys.

  forsake (*v*): to give something up

YOUR TURN

Match the vocab words on the left with the word or phrase that means the opposite on the right.

ARGUMENTS

1.	explicit	a.	docile
2.	pugnacious	b.	blessing
3.	exasperated	c.	with restrictions
4.	benevolent	d.	contented
5.	unconditional	e.	not guilty
6.	resilient	f.	to anger
7.	malediction	g.	unclear
8.	extricate	h.	to make unclear
9.	culpable	i.	weak
10.	placate	j.	to entangle
11.	delineate	k.	unkind

In each of the groups below, choose the word that does not belong.

12. goad   urge   forsake   exhort

13. objective   intuitive   unbiased   disinterested

14. resilience   strength   compassion   fortitude

15. disaffected   contrite   penitent   apologetic

16. chastise   vindicate   admonish   criticize

From the list below, select the word that best describes each person portrayed in the phrases below.

reconciliatory   carping   maternal   interrogatory   vindicated   submissive
rescinding   tentative   obstinate

17.   A person who goes on and on about how much they hate reality television

18. A child who refuses to take a bath
19. A boyfriend who brings his girlfriend flowers after a big fight
20. A person who thinks he'll see the new Farrelly Brothers movie on Saturday, but might change his mind if the reviews are bad
21. A father who waits up till you get home and then asks you a million questions about where you've been all night
22. A kid who always listens to his parents and never questions their authority
23. A kindergarten teacher who always has a kind word and a piece of candy for a kid who scrapes his knees
24. A defendant who wins a trial and is declared not guilty
25. A parent who doesn't let you go out on Friday night, even though last week they promised you could

CHAPTER 18

HOW TO TALK ABOUT A FANCY DANCE

Walter and I arrived at the dance—fashionably late, of course—after a surprisingly civil dinner. I have to hand it to the committee: They did a fantastic job with the decorations. Normally, the Philip J. McCracken Community Center was a total boring dump—think Eagle Scout ceremonies and square dances. But tonight, with the lights low and the decorations up, it looked like a totally different place. The theme was "Rock the Casbah" (which narrowly beat out "Post-Communist Prague" and "The Brady Bunch"), and the whole place was done up in a Middle Eastern theme. The centerpieces were bouquets of peacock feathers, and silhouettes of domes were etched on the walls. The whole place was dripping in gold: streamers, balloons—Janet had even managed to arrange a gold disco ball instead of a silver one. The students weren't about to be outdone by the decorations, either. Some girls had obviously spent more on their formal dresses than I could imagine spending in a *month* of shopping.

Walter and I felt really awkward for a while—this was totally not our scene. We spent the first twenty minutes or so standing by the refreshments, watching as a bunch of punks kept trying to distract Mr. Limbergh, the principal, so they could spike the punch. Finally I'd had enough, so I pulled Walter onto the dance floor. Tom the DJ was spinning a great Jackson Five song, and we threw up our hands and jumped around like a pair of fools. For a second, I thought about how much fun it would have been if Rex had been there with me . . . but then I put it out of my mind. After all, here I was having a great time with someone I once considered my mortal enemy—shouldn't that be enough?

When the song was over, Tom announced that he was taking a short break, but that a friend of his was going to take over for a while. Walter and I were about to head over to get some punch when the microphone let out a loud squawk, followed by a voice that said, "A few weeks ago, a girl did something really gutsy for me. So I guess I'm going to have to return the favor." I turned around to see Rex—

175

wearing a tuxedo and his Converse sneakers—flanked by the rest of the Giants. He gave the audience a sheepish grin. And then the Giants launched into the loudest version of "Hard for Me to Say I'm Sorry," by Chicago, that I think has ever been played on this earth.

Walter and I stood watching the stage; he had a faint grimace on his face, but I could tell he was hiding admiration. "Well, that's pretty stupid. And he's not even a senior. How the hell did he get in?" He looked over at me, and I couldn't hide the fact that I was grinning like an idiot. He let out a loud, dramatic sigh. "Oh, *all right*. There are some chess team kids over there I want to say hi to anyhow. But," he said as he walked off, "if you make out with him, don't expect a ride home."

The Giants ended their song and Rex shuffled off the stage. As he walked toward me, I could sense that every pair of eyes in that place was watching. I forced myself not to blush. Rex, on the other hand, wasn't doing such a good job. "Um, hey," he said.

"Hey," I replied. And then, even though it meant I might have to walk all the way home, I kissed him.

* * * * *

WORDS ABOUT NOT FITTING IN

The idea of me at a formal dance was pretty **farcical**—especially being there with Walter Chen.

farcical (*adj*): resembling a farce; ridiculous and confused

RELATED WORDS

A synonym for *farcical* is **ludicrous** (*adj*): ridiculous.

It quickly became **manifest** that Walter felt as awkward there as I did.
manifest (*adj*): made obvious or clear

We stood near the punch bowls, feeling totally **extraneous**.
extraneous (*adj*): extra and unnecessary

Looking around, I immediately felt **incongruous**.
incongruous (*adj*): strange and out of place

I was sure everyone could sense that I was an **anomaly**. I was **incompatible** with all the people I saw around me. I shouldn't have been so paranoid, though. No one was **ostracizing** me, even though my date was a social **pariah** like Walter.
anomaly (*n*): something that doesn't belong
incompatible (*adj*): unable to blend in or get along
ostracize (*v*): to avoid or exclude someone from a group
pariah (*n*): an outcast

I was proud of the fact that I was wearing my Doc Martens—I hate being a **conformist**!
conformist (*n*): a person who always thinks and behaves in socially acceptable ways

It was all so perfect in there—I kind of wish my brothers were around, so they could do something **disruptive** like set off a cherry bomb in the boys' toilet.
disruptive (*adj*): causing disorder

One girl was wearing a totally **anachronistic** dress that looked like it came from the turn of the century. I had to give her props for being original.
anachronistic (*adj*): from the wrong period of time

When Walter went to the florist to pick up my corsage, he realized there was a **discrepancy** in the order: instead of red roses, the shop had written down orange camellias.
discrepancy (*n*): a difference between two things that are supposed to match

WORDS ABOUT CLOTHING

Some of the girls' dresses were so **embellished** with beads and sequins that it was hard to tell what color the material was underneath.
embellished (*adj*): having lots of ornaments and decorations

A FANCY DANCE

RELATED WORDS

These words all have to do with being fancy or extravagant.

I have to admit, all the **sumptuous** dresses swirling around me were kind of exciting. But I was glad to be wearing my simple dress and not some **baroque** monstrosity. I mean, some of those girls must have paid **exorbitant** prices for their outfits. Some girls managed to look classy and elegant, but lots of others looked **garish** and **gaudy**.

> **sumptuous** (*adj*): luxurious, magnificent
> **baroque** (*adj*): excessively exaggerated in style
> **exorbitant** (*adj*): extravagantly large or high

garish (*adj*) and **gaudy** (*adj*): excessively colorful or shiny, with the added impression of looking fake or cheap

And these words have to do with *not* being fancy or extravagant.

With all those dolled-up girls, I actually felt quite original in my **nondescript** dress. And the sparkly clips in my hair kept me from looking too **austere**.

> **nondescript** (*adj*): plain, uninteresting
> **austere** (*adj*): extremely simple, severely plain

I saw one girl's high heel get caught in the skirt of her **voluminous** dress.

> **voluminous** (*adj*): large, expansive

In general, all the girls looked quite **comely**.

> **comely** (*adj*): pretty, attractive (applies to women)

I especially liked Janet's dress, a **sinuous** silk one that showed off her figure in just the right way.

> **sinuous** (*adj*): slinky, winding

The straps of Janet's dress were covered in **gilt**.

> **gilt** (*n*): a thin layer of gold

Things made of *gilt* would be **lustrous** (*adj*) and **refulgent** (*adj*): both words mean "shiny." *Lustrous* describes a soft shine, *refulgent* a bright one.

Janet **enhanced** her bright green eyes by wearing bright emerald earrings.

> **enhance** (*v*): to improve a particular quality in something

Tara Mickleson, the head cheerleader, was wearing an airy **gossamer** dress that left little to the imagination.

gossamer (*n*): a very thin, filmy material

These words all describe dresses you can see through.

translucent (*adj*): letting light through, but not completely transparent

diaphanous (*adj*): gauzy, delicate

ethereal (*adj*): insubstantial, airy

Obviously, Tara got named Queen of the Formal. When they put all the **regalia** on her, she looked like she was born to be a beauty queen.

regalia (*n*): formal, ceremonial clothing and objects worn by members of royalty (crowns, robes, scepters, etc.)

WORDS ABOUT DECORATIONS

I was amazed at the **opulence** of the whole thing—the decorations must have cost the committee a ton of money.

opulence (*n*): affluence, luxurious splendor

RELATED WORDS

The walls were **resplendent** with gold metallic streamers and pearly balloons. I thought the eight-foot-tall ice sculpture in the shape of our school mascot was a little **ostentatious** and **grandiose**, but other people seemed to like it.

resplendent (*adj*): dazzling in appearance

ostentatious (*adj*): showy, obvious

grandiose (*adj*): magnificent, but often also implies pretentious or unrealistic

I was especially impressed because the community center is usually so **spartan**.

spartan (*adj*): very plain and austere

The ice sculpture was a total **behemoth**—I was worried the table underneath was going to collapse from the weight.

> **behemoth** (*n*): something huge and powerful (The Behemoth is an enormous beast referred to in the Bible.)

The **incandescent** bulbs were covered with frosted shades, which cast a soft glow over the room.

> **incandescent** (*adj*): giving off light

Some synonyms for *incandescent* are **effulgent** (*adj*) and **luminous** (*adj*).

The large, open community center was transformed into a **palatial** space.

> **palatial** (*adj*): spacious and luxurious, like a palace

Some synonyms for *palatial* are **capacious** (*adj*) and **commodious** (*adj*): spacious.

The refreshments table was **replete** with goodies prepared by the Parents Association.

> **replete** (*adj*): fully supplied

There were **copious** amounts of legal, nonalcoholic beverages available.

> **copious** (*adj*): large in quantity

There were clumps of trees outside the community center—a perfect place for lovers' **trysts**.

> **tryst** (*n*): a secret, prearranged meeting, usually between lovers

The parent volunteers were running around **frenetically**, trying to keep kids from spiking the punch.

> **frenetic** (*adj*): frenzied, rushed

The photographer had a palace-themed set for the pictures, but the building itself was just a **façade**—a painted piece of cardboard.

> **façade** (*n*): the outward appearance of something. When used to describe people, it usually implies that there is a *discrepancy* between what is outside and what is inside: "I thought Tara's sweetness was just a *façade*, but it turns out she actually is that nice."

YOUR TURN

Match the vocab words on the left with their definitions on the right.

1.	gilt	a.	clear, apparent
2.	manifest	b.	surface
3.	gaudy	c.	outcast
4.	anachronistic	d.	gold
5.	façade	e.	farcical
6.	tryst	f.	garish
7.	pariah	g.	something that doesn't belong
8.	comely	h.	attractive
9.	ludicrous	i.	of the wrong time period
10.	anomaly	j.	secret meeting

In each of the groups below, choose the word that does not belong.

11. spartan   austere   nondescript   resplendent
12. incandescent   ethereal   effulgent   luminous
13. embellished   baroque   conformist   sumptuous
14. flagrant   capacious   commodious   palatial
15. gossamer   diaphanous   translucent   voluminous

Choose the word that best completes the sentence.

16. The wolf was _____ by the pack after he announced he wanted to become a vegetarian.
    (A) disrupted (B) enhanced (C) embellished (D) ostracized

17. I always feel really _____ at family reunions, because I'm a good six inches taller than most of my relatives.
    (A) flagrant (B) incongruous (C) embellished (D) frenetic

18. My dad used to drive this huge SUV that was a total _____.
    (A) tryst (B) anomaly (C) conformist (D) behemoth

A FANCY DANCE

A FANCY DANCE

19. My friend's dorm room in college was very _____. She didn't even have any pictures on the walls.
    (A) austere (B) ethereal (C) incompatible (D) baroque

20. For the last history assignment, Walter turned in a(n) _____ report on the Cuban Missile Crisis that stretched to seventy pages.
    (A) opulent (B) voluminous (C) incandescent (D) anachronistic

21. There must have been a(n) _____ somewhere: I know I got an A on this paper, but my report card says I got a D.
    (A) façade (B) farce (C) discrepancy (D) behemoth

22. When he took off his hat, it became _____ that he had gotten a really bad haircut.
    (A) ostentatious (B) manifest (C) sinuous (D) commodious

23. I used to go out sometimes with Janet and her then-boyfriend, Hugh. I hate doing that because I feel so _____, like a complete third wheel.
    (A) incandescent (B) flagrant (C) sumptuous (D) extraneous

24. The butterfly's wings were _____.
    (A) ludicrous (B) effulgent (C) exorbitant (D) diaphanous

25. Dr. Dre has a(n) _____ house. I saw it on *Cribs*, and I'm telling you, it's huge.
    (A) palatial (B) frenetic (C) incongruous (D) lustrous

CHAPTER 19

HOW TO TALK ABOUT GRADUATION AND SPEECHES

Strange, I thought to myself, how graduation is always the end of the story.

I was sitting on a hard plastic chair in the bright May sun. Five months had passed since the Winter Formal (or, as Rex and I like to call it, The Night When It All Went Down), and ever since then time had just barreled on—until now, when I found myself in the middle of the football field in a scratchy polyester gown, surrounded by four hundred other people in similarly scratchy gowns. Despite itchy graduation wear, the mood was festive: balloons, beach balls, hysterically crying parents—yup, all the usual.

The graduation speaker that day was our local state senator; from the bored looks around me, I sensed that most people were not thrilled by our administration's choice. (In the last few weeks before graduation, a petition started circulating to have the guy from Blink-182 come instead.) Like most graduation speakers, she was a total windbag android. Blah blah blah, you are the future. Blah blah blah, we expect great things from you. Blah blah blah, take time to stop and smell the roses. Someone started throwing around a beach ball, and I let my mind drift as she droned on.

As class president, Janet was sitting up on the platform with all the administrators. After being accepted everywhere she had applied, she had decided she was going to the college in San Diego. They had offered her that major scholarship, and she was going to go off there to study molecular cellular development of . . . um, something or other. I watched her up there and felt so proud of everything she had accomplished and all that she had ahead of her.

But if I was excited for her, well, I was *really* excited for me. On my dresser at home was a fat envelope filled with airplane tickets. In two months I was flying off to Paris, where I'd do a French program for the first five months. Then, after a trip home for the holidays (Dad insisted), I was going to join a student group that was traveling across Asia, studying art and architecture in China, India, and Nepal. But before all that, I was going to spend two weeks in a tour bus with the Giants, as they launched into their first tour of California—two weeks of being an *Almost Famous*-style groupie sounded like a good way to start my summer. I'd like to think Professor Wexler would be proud of my plans—I'll have to tell Janet to take a class with her for me.

The senator ended her speech in a huff when the beach ball accidentally hit her in the face. Mr. Limbergh, looking all red-faced and angry, announced that because of our awful behavior he was canceling the traditional cap throwing and ending the graduation ceremonies then and there. There was mass confusion as everyone started stampeding out of their seats to go find their families; I narrowly avoided being trampled by a fleet of linebackers. I sighed. So this was going to be my final memory of high school. Fitting, I guess. Lots of confused people running around like morons. As usual.

And you know what? I was kind of going to miss it.

But if you quote me on it, I'll deny it.

* * * * *

WORDS ABOUT ENDINGS AND THE FUTURE

We, the class of 2004, were ready to leave our **callow** days behind.

> **callow** (*adj*): young, inexperienced

Our four years in high school had **transmuted** us from silly, immature children into confident young adults. Supposedly.

> **transmute** (*v*): to change one thing into another, fundamentally different thing

RELATED WORDS

The following words all have to do with change.

All year long, I **vacillated** about what to do after graduation. Should I go to college? Should I travel? I couldn't seem to make up my mind. Now, I hate the notion that teenagers are **capricious** or **fickle**—as a matter of fact, I thought carefully about all my options.

> **vacillate** (*n*): to go back and forth; to be indecisive
> **capricious** (*adj*): fanciful, often changing one's mind suddenly
> **fickle** (*adj*): likely to change one's mind or loyalties

Hopefully, the various lessons I've learned these past eighteen years will make me an **adaptable** person.

> **adaptable** (*adj*): able to change easily in new situation

After all, the future is likely to be **volatile**—I should be ready for anything.

> **volatile** (*adj*): unstable; changing rapidly, unpredictably, and violently

My dad was concerned that I not act **impulsively** while traveling alone—not everyone in the world can be trusted.

> **impulsive** (*adj*): to act without thinking or considering the consequences

I feel like, in the last few months of senior year, time **accelerated** really rapidly—I have no idea how it got to be June already!

> **accelerate** (*v*): to speed up

I don't think my life will follow a certain, **sequential** path. I suspect there are quite a few surprises in my future.

> **sequential** (*adj*): occurring in a certain, progressive order

There are only two **inevitable** things in the world—death and taxes.

> **inevitable** (*adj*): unable to be avoided

High school has **engendered** in me a certain distaste for organized education.

> **engender** (*v*): to bring about, to cause something to be

Graduation gives us an opportunity to celebrate the **consummation** of four years of education.

> **consummation** (*n*): a completion or conclusion

Going to college to become a doctor represents the **realization** of Janet's dreams. Finally, all her studying and planning had come to **fruition**.

realization (*n*))and **fruition** (*n*): the fulfillment of a plan or promise

I found the whole graduation ceremony pretty **anticlimactic**. How was this simple little ceremony supposed to capture all the craziness that is high school?
   anticlimactic (*adj*): an ending that fails to be satisfying or interesting

I've done some pretty stupid things in the last four years, but nothing that causes me true **compunction**—except maybe some of the awful things I've said about Walter.
   compunction (*n*): shame or regret over something you've done

WORDS ABOUT ACCOMPLISHMENT

Janet received many **accolades** at graduation—scholar-athlete, highest GPA, most involved student . . . the list goes on and on.
   accolade (*n*): recognition, award

The following words all have to do with praise.

She was simply showered with **adulation**. If they had wanted to **exalt** her any more, they'd have to build a solid gold statue for her in the quad. I had to **commend** myself for having such a smart best friend (and for not feeling jealous about how everyone wanted to **extol** her). Teachers and administrators had nothing but **laudatory** things to say about her.
   adulation (*n*): very high praise
   exalt (*v*): to raise high
   commend (*v*): to congratulate, to take notice of someone's good work
   extol (*v*): praise highly
   laudatory (*adj*): full of high praise

Sometimes I wish my **aspirations** were as clear and well-defined as Janet's.
   aspiration (*n*): desire to achieve something

But then I think, it took a lot of **initiative** to do what I was doing—no one else was going abroad next year.
   initiative (*n*): the ability to act without the aid of others

I had to be really **industrious** to collect all that information and come up with a plan.

    industrious (*adj*): hard-working

Being the softie he is, my dad teared up as he told me I was quite the **exemplary** young woman.

    exemplary (*adj*): exceptional; of the highest quality

That was a surprise—sometimes I think he finds me **mediocre** at best.

    mediocre (*adj*): average, unexceptional

I tried to **exploit** his sentimental mood by asking for a new car.

    exploit (*v*): to unfairly use something or someone to your own advantage

People who did very well in particular areas were rewarded for their **prowess** at graduation.

    prowess (*n*): outstanding ability, skill

Tara Mickleson won an award for her **facility** with foreign languages—who knew?

    facility (*n*): the ability to do something easily

I was given an award for creative writing, which surprised me so much I almost fell over while walking up to the podium. Luckily, I managed to pick myself up and accept the award with some level of **finesse**.

    finesse (*n*): the ability to do something skillfully and elegantly

The creative writing **citation** is now framed and sitting on top of the piano.

    citation (*n*): an official recognition of accomplishment

Honestly, I think making it out of high school alive is **triumph** enough.

    triumph (*v*): to succeed, especially in the face of enemies or difficulties

At the end of the ceremony, we were each called up individually and had our degrees **bestowed** upon us.

    bestow (*v*): to give something ceremonially

A synonym for *bestow* is **confer** (*v*)).

Now that I had a high school diploma, I had the proper **credentials** for several jobs.

    credentials (*n*): qualifications

GRADUATION AND SPEECHES

Janet and I had the same **verdict** about the graduation ceremonies: utterly, totally boring.

    verdict (*n*): a judgment or decision

WORDS ABOUT SPEECHES

Few politicians these days can really deliver a powerful, moving **oratory**.

    oratory (*n*): a public, usually formal speech

Rhetoric used to be taught in schools as a formal subject, but hardly anyone studies it anymore.

    rhetoric (*n*): the art of using language persuasively

The senator's long, windy **preamble** took almost twenty minutes.

    preamble (*n*): introduction

In it, she quoted the line "I came, I saw, I conquered," which she claimed was said by an **anonymous** speaker. Actually, Julius Caesar said it.

    anonymous (*adj*): not known or identified

She tried to tell a funny **anecdote** about her senior year in high school, but it completely fell flat.

    anecdote (*n*): a short, amusing personal story

She was trying to come across as witty and **glib**, but she just sounded like a stuffy grown-up trying to be hip and cool.

    glib (*adj*): witty and insincere, inappropriately casual

The senator was far from **eloquent**—she kept using the same, boring phrases over and over again and trying to hammer her points home.

    eloquent (*adj*): said expressively and persuasively

She did tell one **poignant** story, though, about being the first person in her family to get a college degree.

    poignant (*adj*): touching, moving

Her **declamatory** style, however, almost ruined the effect. I wished she had just talked like a normal person, instead of like someone Delivering A Big Important Speech.

    declamatory (*adj*): loud and dramatic, but not particularly meaningful

Her **grandiloquence** really got on my nerves. It was as if she were too important to be bothered speaking to a bunch of high schoolers.

    grandiloquence (*adj*): pretentious, overly self-important manner of speaking or writing

RELATED WORDS

Her attempts at more poetic passages came across sounding **euphuistic**.

    euphuistic (*adj*): artificially elegant or refined language

Her speech was incredibly **verbose**; she would always use three words when just one would have done.

    verbose (*adj*): wordy

I wished she had been more **concise**.

    concise (*adj*): brief, to the point

In an attempt to sound intelligent, she peppered her speech with lots of **esoteric** references to classical literature.

    esoteric (*adj*): hard to understand

She also used a lot of political **jargon** that flew over the heads of most of the students.

    jargon (*n*): specialized, usually technical language

It was **promulgated** that she had been paid a large sum of money to speak at our graduation.

    promulgate (*v*): to make something widely known

It was an election year, so the senator was **proselytizing**, hoping to turn some of us potential voters over to her party.

    proselytize (*v*): to preach a particular viewpoint with the hopes of bringing people into one's camp

GRADUATION AND SPEECHES

YOUR TURN

Match the vocab words on the left with the word or phrase that means the opposite on the right.

1.	mediocre	a.	verbose
2.	vacillate	b.	easy to understand
3.	eloquent	c.	calm
4.	concise	d.	lazy
5.	esoteric	e.	extraordinary
6.	exalt	f.	avoidable
7.	volatile	g.	to be decisive
8.	inevitable	h.	defeat
9.	industrious	i.	poorly spoken
10.	triumph	j.	criticize

Choose the best word from the list given below to fill in the blanks. Not every word will be used.

realization   rhetoric   bestow   anonymous   facility   jargon   accolade
industrious   anecdote   credentials   poignant   preamble   exemplary   extol
initiative   esoteric   verdict   impulsive   oratory   promulgate   exploit   glib

11. Janet and I made a(n) _____ decision to drive down to San Diego one Friday morning.
12. Seeing her movie win the Academy Award for best picture was the _____ of a lifelong dream.
13. The Academy Award is the greatest _____ a filmmaker can receive.
14. For his _____ work in film throughout the years, Jack Nicholson was given a Lifetime Achievement Award.
15. Because of her _____ with computers, Tasha wanted to get a job as a software engineer.
16. Donald is a master of _____; give him ten minutes, and he can convince anyone to do anything.

17. I wanted to work at the city newspaper, but unfortunately I didn't have the proper _____ for a job like that: usually, you need at least three years of experience on a college newspaper first.

18. In his article, the reporter plans to _____ the fact that the whole Academy Awards ceremony was fixed.

19. The _____ story about the little boy and his dying dog brought a tear to my eye.

20. I hate reading articles in technical magazines, because they are always filled with scientific _____ that I don't understand.

21. My history teacher likes to start every class with a funny _____ about his five-year-old daughter, Olivia.

22. It makes for a nice, introductory _____ to the class itself.

23. I cannot _____ the virtues of Ben and Jerry's Chunky Monkey ice cream too highly. It really is the perfect food product.

24. Rowan is a graduate student who writes about all kinds of _____ books. Just looking at those things give me a headache, but she seems to understand it all.

25. When I found out that my brothers had been cutting math class regularly, they begged me not to tell Dad. I decided to _____ my new knowledge, and forced them to do my chores for a month.

HᴧPT R ?--
EPILOGUE

July 17
Seattle, WA

Janet—

The rock 'n' roll lifestyle is treating me well. I like sleeping till eleven every morning, but the whole communal van-living thing is harder to take. The Giants Summer Tour 2004 has passed through four cities, but Seattle is my favorite so far. We should definitely move here once you graduate—lots of water, lots of trees, lots of coffee shops. (This postcard is from the first Starbucks in the whole United States! That probably shouldn't excite me as much as it does.) Hope you're doing well and are getting all psyched for school in the fall. I'll be home before you leave—we need to do at least one more horror movie marathon before you go! But please—let's avoid the whole road-trip-encounters-a-serial-killer genre, shall we?

Love,
Alex

* * * * *

October 30
Paris, France

Dear Dad:

Bonjour from beautiful Paris! I just wanted to drop you a postcard to tell you I am having a safe, productive, educational time in France. Today on our orientation, we toured around to all the big tourist spots in Paris, and I bought this card from the Eiffel Tower. It was fun, but I can't wait to get out on my own and see all

195

this city has to offer. I'm excited to sit in little cafes and scribble in journals all day. Just think! Maybe I'll have produced my big novel by the end of this term. Or else I'll just get fat on all the croissants and pastries I've been downing.

Thanks for the big box of winter clothes. I especially appreciated how each piece was vacuum-sealed and labeled. And no, I don't need anything from home. Stop worrying!!! I will be fine. I'll see you over the holidays.

Tell Mike and Wayne to stay out of my room while I'm gone!

Love,
Alex

*   *   *   *   *

February 13
New Delhi, India

Dear Rex—

Hey you! The group just got to India. I've been spending the afternoon poring over my little Hindi phrasebook—so far I can order a plate of mangoes and ask where the nearest public toilet is. I'm hoping the learning curve gets steeper soon. We're setting off for Agra in a few days to see the Taj Mahal, which I'm really stoked about. We met all these funny hippies on the plane ride over who were headed there, too—I hope we see them when we're there. Hippies crack me up.

Hey! I have a great idea for the Giants' new single. It should be about a globe-trotting girl. Isn't that a catchy title? It would be huge in Asia, I swear.

Hope senior year is treating you well. Don't think about it too much—I promise you, that's the only way to get through it. Enjoy it while it lasts!

Love,
Alex

*   *   *   *   *

WORDS TAKEN FROM FOREIGN LANGUAGES

FRENCH

I'm not much of an athlete, but I loved the **esprit de corps** of playing on a soccer team.

> **esprit de corps** (*n*): spirit of being a team

When I'm famous, I'll have a great **nom de plume**—Alex Lee just doesn't cut it.

> **nom de plume** (*n*): a name used by a writer instead of his or her real name (pen name)

I hate to admit it, but I love Pink—I think she dresses with such **élan**. You gotta love all that leather!

> **élan** (*n*): enthusiasm, self-confidence, and style

In three months, though, she's going to look totally **passé**.

> **passé** (*adj*): outdated, out of fashion

Reading at the Tin Cup is great because of the **bonhomie**—everyone is just there to have a good time.

> **bonhomie** (*n*): good-natured friendliness

At this point, I've read nearly my entire **oeuvre** at the Cup. I'm going to have to come up with some new poems soon.

> **oeuvre** (*n*): body of work

Janet is the ultimate in **savoir-faire**. Doesn't matter if she's with administrators, fellow students, or screaming eight-year-olds at her volunteer job: somehow, she's brilliant with everyone.

> **savoir-faire** (*n*): the ability to act capably in any situation

As rowdy as my brothers get, they do have a certain **joie de vivre** that is pretty appealing.

> **joie de vivre** (*n*): a joy in living

My dad's signature dish is Everything Stew—which is pretty much just a **mélange** of whatever is left in the fridge.

    mélange (*n*): a mixture of different kinds of things

Whenever I see Rex, I'm terrified of committing a **faux pas**—like accidentally spitting in his eye while saying hello.

    faux pas (*n*): an act that is socially awkward

I'd love to be Professor Wexler's **protégé** and eventually have a career just like hers.

    protégé (*n*): a young person guided by an older person of more experience or influence

My novel—whenever it gets finished—will be hailed as a **tour de force**.

    tour de force (*n*): something done brilliantly

When the first N'Sync album came out, all my junior high friends and I went **en masse** to buy it.

    en masse (*adj*): many people acting as one

LATIN

Walter Chen is such an **agitator**—he hates a dull classroom.

    agitator (*n*): one who stirs up trouble

He's annoying, but he's not exactly **sinister**. It's hard to intimidate someone you knew as a fourth grader.

    sinister (*adj*): wicked, threatening

Whenever my brothers compliment me, I'm worried that they have an **ulterior** motive. What do they want from me?

    ulterior (*adj*): lying underneath

Everything's **quid pro quo** with them; like, we'll walk the dog if you do the dishes.

    quid pro quo (*n*): done with the expectation that something will be done in return

Their **modus operandi** is to never do anything for free.

    modus operandi (*n*): way of doing things

I got Janet **premium** tickets to the Boredoms concert for her birthday.

    premium (*adj*): the best quality

I am a **bona fide** best friend.
> **bona fide** (*adj*): genuine

Last year, Janet's birthday was a totally **ad hoc** deal—we all forgot about it, and had to put together a pizza party at the last minute.
> **ad hoc** (*adj*): done without much preparation, usually just for the situation at hand

At big school deals, I always feel like a total **persona non grata**. After all, I'm not a jock, a cheerleader, or any kind of class superstar. Why would anyone want me around?
> **persona non grata** (*n*): an unwelcome or unacceptable person

I don't hate high school **per se**; I can just think of better things to do with my time.
> **per se** (*adv*): by itself, in itself

ITALIAN

My dad's voice always reaches a huge **crescendo** as he yells at my brothers.
> **crescendo** (*n*): a gradual increase in volume

When my mom got angry, she'd never yell—but you could always tell she was angry when she started talking in **staccato**.
> **staccato** (*n*): done in a very quick rhythm; clipped

Usually, my mother spoke at a very easy, soothing **tempo**.
> **tempo** (*n*): the speed at which something is sung or spoken

The head cheerleader is a total **prima donna**. She always expects people to carry her books and fall at her feet.
> **prima donna** (*n*): a conceited person with a big ego. The term is taken from opera, and means "the main female soloist."

HINDI

Senior year is a total **juggernaut**; you just can't stop it from barreling you over.
> **juggernaut** (*n*): something huge, crushing, and unstoppable

A kid from my school got busted for **looting** a 7-Eleven.
> **loot** (*v*): to steal, especially during wartime

I can see Walter growing up to be a television political **pundit**, loudly giving advice that no one cares about.

pundit (*n*): someone who is an authority on a particular subject

GERMAN

Thinking about all my homework used to fill me with **angst**.

angst (*n*): dread and anxiety

Due to their **schadenfreude**, my brothers got a kick out of watching me struggle with senior year.

schadenfreude (*n*): taking joy in other people's pain

They'll continue to **shirk** their work all through high school, I bet.

shirk (*v*): to avoid work or responsibility

My brothers' coolness is only a thin **veneer**—underneath it all, they're still dorks who used to play Magic: The Gathering.

veneer (*n*): a thin outer layer

GREEK

Sometimes I like reading *Vogue* magazine and checking out all the **aristocrats**, but most of the time I'm perfectly happy living in the suburbs and being middle class.

aristocrat (*n*): member of the upper class

The **genesis** of my love for poetry was in eighth grade, when I found a book by e.e. cummings.

genesis (*n*): the beginning, the origin

Janet's **myopia** forces her to wear glasses.

myopia (*n*): nearsightedness

I had **myriad** options for the year after graduation: I could go to college, I could get a job, I could backpack through Europe. . . .

myriad (*adj*): made of many different elements

The day we graduated, the whole school erupted in **pandemonium**.

pandemonium (*n*): wild chaos

From my backyard, you can look out and see a **panorama** of the city.
   panorama (*n*): wide, sweeping view

Walter's always gripped with **paranoia**—he thinks everyone's out to get him.
   paranoia (*n*): extreme anxiety and suspicion

After reading the **synopsis** of that sappy new film, I think I've heard enough to avoid it.
   synopsis (*n*): a brief summary of a story

DUTCH

The popular kids at school like to **jeer** at all the uncool kids.
   jeer (*n*): to sneer at, to mock

My attempts at making Everything Stew resulted in a disgusting **morass**.
   morass (*n*): sticky mess

I had to **scour** the pot for a good fifteen minutes with a steel wool pad.
   scour (*v*): to clean by rubbing vigorously

My dad says I should stop **ranting** so much and actually go accomplish something.
   rant (*v*): to complain loudly and at length

YIDDISH

Janet had the **chutzpah** to ask Rex for his phone number for me.
   chutzpah (*n*): daring, confidence, and impudence

The made-for-TV movie's **schmaltz** made me want to retch.
   schmaltz (*n*): something that is sickly in its sentimentality

SPANISH

Whenever I'm writing a new poem, I **barricade** my door so my family can't bother me.
   barricade (*n*): something built to block access

After the mad cow scare, many governments placed **embargos** on the importation of American beef.

    embargo (*n*): a government restriction on commerce

PERSIAN

When the Giants went on tour, they took three cars and traveled in a **caravan**.

    caravan (*n*): a group of vehicles traveling together

I bought Janet a set of gold bangles from a **bazaar** in India.

    bazaar (*n*): outdoor street market

YOUR TURN

Match the vocab words on the left with their definitions on the right.

1.	esprit de corps	a.	joyousness
2.	joie de vivre	b.	beginning
3.	sinister	c.	enjoying other people's misfortunes
4.	crescendo	d.	spirit of teamwork
5.	schadenfreude	e.	blockade
6.	synopsis	f.	the highest quality
7.	barricade	g.	the loudest point
8.	premium	h.	thin outer layer
9.	veneer	i.	brief summary
10.	genesis	j.	wicked

The descriptions below provide examples of these vocabulary terms. Match the description with the proper phrase.

bonhomie   protégé   agitator   tour de force   quid pro quo   persona non grata
prima donna   juggernaut   pundit   aristocrat   pandemonium   paranoia
morass   chutzpah   schmaltz

11. A person who spreads rumors about other people, hoping that it'll result in a really great lunchtime fight

12. A Hollywood star who refuses to shower with anything but Evian water, and insists that crewmembers refer to her as "Your Majesty"

13. A huge pool of tar, spilled on the side of the road

14. A political expert who explains Congressional matters on CNN

15. A person who is always convinced that the government is tapping her phone

16. A novel that is hailed as "the greatest novel of the new millennium"

17. The son of a wealthy senator, who attends the best private schools and has his own yacht

18. The Giants on tour, spending lots of time laughing and playing video games

19. Mike telling Wayne that he'll write Wayne's English essay if Wayne does his chem homework

20. When the lights accidentally go out at a concert, and everyone in the audience goes into a panic

21. A sentimental movie about a dog saving a young boy from drowning.

22. The Giants marching into the offices of a major record label and telling the record executive that they're the best band he's never heard, and that he should sign them

23. The wallflower that stands in the corner at the dance, being ignored by all the cool kids

24. An eager young reporter who is being trained to be a great journalist by an older, more established writer

25. A huge Humvee that can flatten small cities under its tires

ANSWER KEY

CHAPTER 1

1. i
2. a
3. h
4. e
5. j
6. g
7. d
8. b
9. c
10. f
11. mordant
12. disheveled
13. defiance
14. threatening
15. imperturbable
16. c
17. b
18. d
19. a
20. b
21. b
22. d
23. c
24. a
25. d

CHAPTER 2

1. a
2. i
3. d
4. e
5. f

6. g
7. j
8. h
9. c
10. b
11. unintelligent
12. greedy
13. stubborn
14. lazy
15. inspired
16. c
17. a
18. d
19. a
20. a
21. b
22. d
23. c
24. b
25. a

CHAPTER 3

1. h
2. c
3. f
4. i
5. d
6. e
7. j
8. b
9. a
10. g
11. weaken
12. aloofness

13. boredom
14. praise
15. silent
16. c
17. b
18. d
19. a
20. b
21. a
22. d
23. c
24. a
25. c

CHAPTER 4

1. colorful
2. affluent
3. effortless
4. revolting
5. similar
6. similar
7. different
8. different
9. different
10. similar
11. redolent
12. corpulent
13. stultifying
14. malodorous
15. diligent
16. bereft
17. affluence
18. epicurean
19. glutton

20. coagulate
21. dreg
22. abysmal
23. strenuous
24. interminable
25. unparalleled

CHAPTER 5

1. different
2. different
3. similar
4. similar
5. different
6. similar
7. similar
8. similar
9. similar
10. different
11. c
12. d
13. a
14. d
15. c
16. a
17. b
18. d
19. a
20. b
21. c
22. a
23. c
24. b
25. a

CHAPTER 6

1. p
2. m
3. h
4. k
5. l
6. f
7. b
8. e
9. j
10. c
11. i
12. d
13. o
14. g
15. a
16. n
17. compliment
18. definitive
19. censure
20. equitable
21. dissemble
22. abrogate
23. elude
24. complement
25. continuous

CHAPTER 7

1. g
2. c
3. j
4. e
5. h

6. i
7. f
8. b
9. d
10. a
11. impervious
12. congregation
13. bashful
14. mellifluous
15. symphonic
16. c
17. a
18. d
19. b
20. a
21. d
22. c
23. b
24. a
25. d

CHAPTER 8

1. similar
2. different
3. similar
4. different
5. similar
6. similar
7. similar
8. different
9. different
10. different
11. perspicacity
12. praise

13. erudite
14. acquiescent
15. savvy
16. b
17. c
18. a
19. a
20. d
21. b
22. c
23. b
24. a
25. c

CHAPTER 9

1. i
2. g
3. j
4. b
5. c
6. h
7. a
8. d
9. e
10. f
11. relaxed
12. anger
13. perfunctory
14. consternation
15. palliate
16. serene
17. timorous
18. impeccable
19. disparaging

20. unequivocal
21. devious
22. loitering
23. assuaging
24. perfunctory
25. arbitrary

CHAPTER 10

1. similar
2. different
3. different
4. similar
5. similar
6. different
7. similar
8. different
9. different
10. similar
11. compatible
12. connubial
13. furtive
14. impetuous
15. histrionic
16. b
17. c
18. a
19. d
20. b
21. d
22. a
23. d
24. c
25. a

CHAPTER 11

1. f
2. i
3. g
4. b
5. a
6. d
7. h
8. j
9. e
10. c
11. hallowed
12. unassailable
13. incorrigible
14. precocious
15. obsequious
16. abdicate
17. venerable
18. cull
19. profane
20. bilk
21. longevity
22. insatiable
23. bequeath
24. avid
25. amenities

CHAPTER 12

1. d
2. k
3. n
4. e
5. c

6. h
7. b
8. i
9. l
10. o
11. p
12. g
13. j
14. f
15. m
16. a
17. odious
18. stimulant
19. imminent
20. unexceptionable
21. cite
22. absolve
23. incredulous
24. odorous
25. plenitude

CHAPTER 13

1. similar
2. similar
3. different
4. different
5. similar
6. similar
7. different
8. similar
9. different
10. similar
11. traverse
12. agitate

13. nomad
14. c
15. d
16. a
17. c
18. b
19. c
20. d
21. a
22. b
23. d
24. d
25. b

CHAPTER 14

1. g
2. d
3. a
4. i
5. b
6. j
7. e
8. c
9. h
10. f
11. strengthen
12. open
13. demonstration
14. gorging
15. chance
16. inoculation
17. abate
18. accomplice
19. clandestine

20. ruse
21. malaise
22. unguent
23. supine
24. cannibal
25. sordid

CHAPTER 15

1. similar
2. similar
3. different
4. different
5. different
6. similar
7. different
8. different
9. similar
10. different
11. desolate
12. flabbergasted
13. treacherous
14. composed
15. mortified
16. mercurial
17. c
18. b
19. d
20. d
21. a
22. d
23. c
24. c
25. b

CHAPTER 16

1. g
2. l
3. d
4. i
5. a
6. k
7. b
8. h
9. c
10. e
11. j
12. f
13. rent
14. lachrymose
15. cupidity
16. pulchritude
17. bumptious
18. infamous
19. logorrhea
20. quixotic
21. rheumy
22. salubrious
23. tyro
24. spendthrift
25. restive

CHAPTER 17

1. g
2. a
3. d
4. k
5. c

6. i
7. b
8. j
9. e
10. f
11. h
12. forsake
13. intuitive
14. compassion
15. disaffected
16. vindicate
17. carping
18. obstinate
19. reconciliatory
20. tentative
21. interrogatory
22. submissive
23. maternal
24. vindicated
25. rescinding

CHAPTER 18

1. d
2. a
3. f
4. i
5. b
6. j
7. c
8. h
9. e
10. g
11. resplendent
12. ethereal

13. conformist
14. flagrant
15. voluminous
16. d
17. b
18. d
19. a
20. b
21. c
22. b
23. d
24. d
25. a

CHAPTER 19

1. e
2. g
3. i
4. a
5. b
6. j
7. c
8. f
9. d
10. h
11. impulsive
12. realization
13. accolade
14. exemplary
15. facility
16. rhetoric
17. credentials
18. promulgate
19. poignant

20. jargon
21. anecdote
22. preamble
23. extol
24. esoteric
25. exploit

CHAPTER 20

1. d
2. a
3. j
4. g
5. c
6. i
7. e
8. f
9. h
10. b
11. agitator
12. prima donna
13. morass
14. pundit
15. paranoia
16. tour de force
17. aristocrat
18. bonhomie
19. quid pro quo
20. pandemonium
21. schmaltz
22. chutzpah
23. persona non grata
24. protégé
25. juggernaut